THE AMAZON VENDOR CENTRAL SELLING GUIDE

Our Blueprint to Growing Your Vendor Central Sales

AMZ Advisers

About AMZ Advisers

AMZ Advisers is a full-service eCommerce & digital marketing consultancy with extensive experience in creating high-growth strategies for brands and manufacturers on the Amazon platform. We partner with companies looking to realize their full eCommerce potential. In 2016, our partners enjoyed $20,000,000+ in sales with many of our partners experiencing more than 100% increase in their year-over-year sales on the Amazon platform.

We believe that developing a robust eCommerce presence is integral for a business looking to maximize growth in the 21st century. Our custom strategies aim to make Amazon, the largest eCommerce marketplace, a powerful sales channel and the centerpiece of every company's eCommerce presence. Long-term growth requires developing alternative sales channels, and we compliment every client's eCommerce strategy by bringing them to additional eCommerce platforms, developing powerful sales funnels and creating websites designed to convert shoppers into customers.

CONTENTS

INTRODUCTION

Amazon has continued to grow its shopper base by unprecedented rates and create incredible, new opportunities for businesses. The eCommerce retail giant has become the go-to starting point for customers searching to buy products online. Small businesses and multinational corporations alike stand to benefit massively from being on the platform. However, many are being left behind from not understanding how the platform works, not using the most cost-effective and efficient ways to grow on Amazon, or not having a presence on the platform at all. Our Amazon blueprint can help any business increase their sales and realize their full potential on this incredible platform.

This book is a culmination of our years of work on the Amazon platform. Through selling products ourselves and growing our clients' sales, we have discovered the most cost-effective and efficient ways to utilize the Amazon platform. Our failures and successes have guided us along the way to creating these powerful strategies. The focus of all our efforts has been to find the best ways to help our clients and to bring them the greatest value possible. We are proud that our custom strategies have helped our clients consistently hit goals and reach entirely new heights for their businesses.

In 2016, our clients broke the $20,000,000 mark for total sales on the Amazon platform. Considering total sales across all platforms, our clients achieved more than $33,000,000 in total sales. We love diving into a business and finding the best ways to grow their business quickly. Our clients averaged 67% growth over prior year sales and our largest clients achieved over 150% growth – some in as little as 5 months – during 2016. Our strategies are constantly evolving and we will continue to search for new growth avenues for our clients' products.

We've designed this book to be the ultimate reference guide for every person or business interested in growing their eCommerce sales. The book certainly can be read section by section, but is designed to provide valuable advice and insight into specific topics around the Amazon platform. Feel free to read the entire book, or flip to sections that are relevant for the platform and stage that your business is at. These strategies work best for established businesses looking to scale, but implementing any of these strategies will take your business to the next level no matter where you currently are.

We hope that you take advantage of our tips and insights into the Amazon platform to realize your company's full eCommerce potential!

Part 1:
Selling on Amazon General Topics

The Amazon Marketplace in 2017

The Amazon marketplace took the eCommerce world by storm in 2016, and its upward trend is not likely to abate this year. Amazon has been pushing hard in the last decade, and has made impressive strides every year since its expansion from its humble beginnings as an online bookstore. This year, the dominant internet retailer is expected to extend its global reach, expand into physical shops around the US, and dive further into focused logistics, AI and entertainment efforts.

New Amazon Marketplace Options

As more and more sellers join the Amazon marketplace to enjoy low-risk eCommerce debuts and high-profit business expansion with this well-established platform, growth for the internet retailer is inevitable. Amazon completed a massive Prime Day promotion last year which pulled in record membership sign-ups and boosted mid-year sales. They have obviously been gearing up for a big year, in which seller expansion into new international markets plays a big part.

The US and Europe

For US sellers to be able to take their offerings to the world, Amazon opened avenues to over 70 countries. Amazon US sellers are also tapped into Canada and Mexico with the North American unified account option, and can enter the European market as well with the more recent European unified account. Europe is the second largest Amazon marketplace after the US, encompassing France, Germany, Italy, Spain, and the UK and representing a potential market of 300 million shoppers.

To attract more global sellers, the platform has been working on opening local sites in several countries. With these options looming large, now is the time for sellers to prepare to expand internationally to take advantage of this open road to success. A single account in one European country allows sellers to warehouse in this one location and take advantage of FBA services to cater to the entire European market.

China, India, and Beyond

Amazon has also launched efforts to enter China and India. China is proving to be difficult with strong local pressure against foreign companies, but the platform has succeeded in attracting a lot of Chinese sellers with their Dragon Boat program. Chinese merchants can easily move their inventory into FBA with special added privileges to help them along the way.

Struggles with Indian regulatory issues are also hindering the eCommerce giant's entry. Intensified efforts are working to grow that market, and this year may be the year that the Amazon marketplace breaks through. Amazon has invested heavily in India, and the company is poised to pour in another 3 billion US dollars to push its expansion there. The addition of Prime Video is only one of the perks that new subscription packages will include.

Australia could be the new Amazon marketplace of the year following the company's search there for warehouse space. Amazon already has one warehouse in Brazil, and this could be the next marketplace in line, despite barriers such as protective customs and high import duties.

Getting Physical

Amazon began as an online retailer to provide an alternative to traditional bookstores. The online giant has since evolved into a diverse marketplace, and is now back on the ground with their pioneering Amazon Go grocery. This 1,800 square foot swipe-and-go store is not your traditional brick and mortar shop, but offers a tech-aided shopping experience that does away with the need for dragging items to a cashier and standing in line to pay. Still a major retail opportunity, Business Insider reported that Amazon has plans of opening another 19 Go stores across the US in 2017 and 2018, plus perhaps as many as 2000 Amazon Fresh stores by 2027. Amazon books has also gone back to basics with the opening of four bookstores that feature test areas for their branded hardware like Kindle. This year will be the year this physical expansion truly takes off.

Logistics Takeover

Amazon has spent the last decade building a truly impressive logistics system. Billions of dollars go into shipping costs each quarter, and this number is continuously rising as the internet retailer drives to deliver faster and to more consumers. Their recent efforts to overtake courier services has led business analysts to believe that Amazon is planning a grand logistics takeover. Amazon is currently leasing trucks, planes, and ships, and has not given up on their drone delivery project.

Disruption Magazine says that Amazon is not only trying to manage all shipping internally, but attempting to launch an app resembling Uber to connect trucks and shippers. This would put Amazon in the running against Uber acquired trucking service Otto. Both companies plan to expand their offerings to shipping by sea and air. The plan would save Amazon over a billion dollars every year. Combined with Amazon's plans to open physical stores around the country, this massive shipping endeavor could also target other retailers in need of logistics services.

As the company takes care of more and more of its own door-to-door deliveries, shipping costs are bound to fall. The free shipping minimum on Amazon.com has already been inconspicuously lowered to 35 US dollars. As the system develops, Amazon's logistics app will integrate pricing, routes and stops while saving on third-part commissions.

Amazon AI

Amazon launched its nifty AI virtual assistant Alexa over two years ago, and its hardware counterpart Echo has been recently upgraded. Before Google and Apple even began with their own versions of this high-tech voice-controlled helper, Amazon was already working on its system to answer customer questions, order products and play music. To maintain its edge over the competition, Amazon has over 1000 people stepping up efforts to keep Alexa fresh, and get this proprietary AI into third-party devices such as the GE smart lamp. Tech Crunch reported in November last year that Amazon was ready to launch its AI platform to bring the technology to outside developers. There are currently three Amazon AI tools available – Rekognition, Amazon Polly, and Lex – but the company has definite plans of adding more over the next several years.

Media Changes

The Amazon marketplace has been offering video on demand since 2008, but has big plans of expanding its service by tripling its current library within the year. The online retail leader has been acquiring a large volume of original movies, TV series and documentaries in an apparent bid to compete with content streaming giants Netflix and Apple. Amazon began offering its video-only monthly subscription plan just last month, expanding the service outside of the Amazon Prime membership.

Amazon has made good on its announcement in November 2016 to implement changes in shipping rates, Buy Box eligibility and media fees by March 1ˢᵗ of this year. To start off, sellers in the media categories now have the freedom to set their own shipping rates by region and even offer free shipping for standard delivery. Sellers also enjoy the ability to compete for the Buy Box for all books sold in new condition. Finally, Amazon has changed the Variable Closing Fees to a fixed fee of 1.80 US dollars per item, and calculates the Referral fee based on the total sales price of an item rather than a percentage of its sales price These changes can push sales for new books up while evening up the competition with Amazon and publishers for the buy box, but used books sellers are going to face even tighter profit margins.

More Smiles All Around

All in all, things are looking up for Amazon and Amazon marketplace sellers this year. There are new avenues of opportunity that sellers can take hold of right away, and more to look forward to throughout the year. This expansion and the renewed focus on logistics also raises hopes that Amazon will be a stable platform on which to establish long-term business ventures. Sellers on and off the platform can also consider expanding from online sales to getting their products in Amazon Go stores at this early stage. Media retail might not be too hot, but lowered shipping fees could take the edge off. On the other hand, the competition generated by Amazon's video efforts is going to be great for content producers and consumers.

How to Rank for Keywords on Amazon

Every seller faces the challenge of getting their products ranking on Amazon. Identifying the main keywords that will convert is vital to sustained Amazon success. Ranking for those keywords is an entirely different battle. We've worked with some of the largest brands to optimize Amazon listings, develop, and implement strategies that will improve their Amazon ranking. Taking the steps below has worked for our clients and will help you rank for keywords on Amazon.

Creating SEO Copywriting for Your Listings

The first to step to rank for keywords on Amazon is to introduce keyword rich content into your Amazon product listings. Amazon's A9 algorithm tries to rank products by their relevancy for each keyword. Creating titles, bullet points and product descriptions that contain the most relevant keywords is the key to improve your Amazon ranking.

Start by researching the most relevant keywords to your products by using tools like Keyword Inspector or Google Keyword Planner. Keyword Inspector is a great tool you can use to crawl your competitors' listings to determine what keywords they are ranking for. It provides a detailed list of keywords that are in the listings and where they currently show up in search engine results pages (SERPs). Google Keyword Planner can also provide great keywords; however, the results are more focused on internet searches and contain keywords not necessarily relevant to a shopping platform like Amazon.

Develop titles, bullet points and product descriptions that use your competitors' top keywords. We recommend using the bullet points to focus on a product's benefits rather than their features. Focusing on product benefits shows shoppers how this product can benefit their lives and can be useful for converting them to customers. As you develop a sales history, Amazon will index you for these keywords on SERPs.

Ranking Products through Sales History

Having the right keywords is the first step to rank for keywords on Amazon. Developing the sales history will increase your visibility on SERPs. The A9 algorithm determines product relevancy by ordered units, conversion rates, click-through rates and product price. All these items are related and it can be difficult to separate how one change influences product rankings on Amazon. We first recommend picking a price that is below the average price of all the products on page 1 for the specific keyword you want to rank for and sticking with that price. Fixing this variable at a specific price will help you identify changes in the other metrics.

Now we can focus on improving the sales history. We recommend starting with discounted products to develop your sales history. Amazon's new seller terms of service indicate that giving products away for reviews is illegal. However, you still can offer discounts to drive traffic. Try creating a promotional discount that you believe will entice shoppers and market that offering through your social media channels or an email list. This can be done by sharing the offer with your current followers and/or, if you don't currently have much of a social media following, running advertisements on Facebook, Twitter and Instagram. Discounted sales still appear to hold equal weight to a full price sale and will begin to build your sales history.

Amazon should begin to index you for the main keywords in your content with these initial sales. The next step we recommend taking is to create automatic advertising campaigns on Amazon. Running these campaigns will make your products appear for the keywords in your listing as well as related keywords that shoppers may be searching for. This will lead to increased sales and provide you important feedback on what other keywords you should consider introducing into the front-end of your listing.

A final step that you can use to rank for keywords on Amazon would be to introduce manual advertising campaigns with Bid+ active. Bid+ is a feature that will increase the maximum cost per click (CPC) bid that are eligible to appear at the top of SERPs. The maximum increase is 50%. For example, say you are currently bidding $1 for a keyword and the top bidder is bidding $1.25. If you have Bid+ active, it will increase your bid up to a $1.50 CPC and your ad will be appearing at the top of the SERP versus your competitor's. Bid+ campaigns can be expensive to run, but are a great way to get conversions on the main keywords you are trying to rank for. Expect higher ACOS and a lower ROI from Bid+ campaigns, but the benefit will hopefully be increased organic sales as your product listing continues to be indexed by Amazon.

Resources

Google Keyword Planner
Free keyword research tool that can provide valuable insight to high traffic keywords on the Google Search Engine
www.adwords.google.com/KeywordPlanner

Keyword Inspector
A keyword research tool developed for Amazon sellers that focuses on finding the keywords that customers use while searching for a product or niche
www.keywordinspector.com

Sellics
A suite of tools that offers a free trial and is designed to help research keywords, optimize listings and grow your business
www.sellics.com

The 4 Amazon Product Ranking Algorithm Factors You Can Impact

Many sellers are feeling slighted by Amazon lately. Policy changes to the product review guidelines have changed strategies. Using discounted products to drive reviews and increase customer conversions are no longer possible. We've been saying since the change that the only way to be successful now is to increase your sales. Amazon is attempting to help with the reviews, but how can you as a seller increase your sales? One simple change that you need to test out can impact the Amazon product ranking algorithm in your favor. We are going to go through a case study of a few changes we made for a client and how it ranked them on Amazon.

The Most Important Factors

Amazon's A9 algorithm is governed by a few main rules and have a single goal in mind; to provide the most relevant results and best deals for their customers. The A9 algorithm only uses data on the Amazon database to determine product relevancy, and does not consider relevancy factors that search engines like Google look for (i.e., backlinks, off-page SEO). Amazon wants to maximize revenue per customer. It therefore tracks all customer data from what they search for to what products they click on after searching to what product they end up buying.

In our experience, there are 4 main factors that can increase product relevancy in the Amazon A9 algorithm. The most important factor is **sales history**. Amazon will index your product based on the search terms present in the listing and how many sales you get on each search term. Getting sales on search terms is a huge indication to Amazon that your product is relevant to the customers' search. It is important to optimize Amazon listings with search terms that are relevant to your product. Too often we see clients going after random keywords that are barely related to their product. Amazon will index for those random keywords and it ends up hurting the seller because the second factor is negatively impacted.

Conversion rates play a very important role in your product's ranking. Converting on a specific search term is another massive relevancy signal for the Amazon A9 algorithm. We've seen through our experience how conversion rates can help boost your product's visibility and we will share that with you. Therefore, focusing on keywords directly related to your product is incredibly important. You will end up killing your conversion rates by going after random keywords that are only slightly related to your product. Similarly, **click thru rate** is relevancy signal that Amazon values. Customer's clicking on your product listing shows product relevancy for the search term. While still important, we believe it is much more important to convert that click into a sale as much as possible.

The final factor is **pricing**, and it's the only factor that you can control. As we said, Amazon wants to show the most relevant results and best deals for the clients. We've noticed that pricing below market averages can give you a huge initial boost to your product. By testing out new pricing strategies you can impact the Amazon product ranking algorithm in your favor.

Case Study: Pricing's Impacts on a Product Listing

We recently worked with a client that launched a product in early January 2016. The product was launched at an above market average price. Initially, the product did not start moving until they dropped the price down a few weeks later. In the chart below you will notice that as they decreased price, page views, orders and conversions increased:

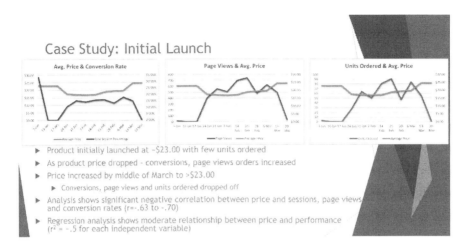

Case Study: Initial Launch

- ▶ Product initially launched at ~$23.00 with few units ordered
- ▶ As product price dropped - conversions, page views orders increased
- ▶ Price increased by middle of March to >$23.00
  - ▶ Conversions, page views and units ordered dropped off
- ▶ Analysis shows significant negative correlation between price and sessions, page views and conversion rates (r=-.63 to -.70)
- ▶ Regression analysis shows moderate relationship between price and performance (r² = -.5 for each independent variable)

These increases are directly related to the product becoming more visible on Amazon. Maintaining a consistent price continued to increase these factors. As the client began to run out of inventory, they started increasing price. The result was a drop in all 3 of those factors. The client killed their conversion rates by increasing the price and thus product visibility decreased drastically. The interesting thing is that even as they decreased price in the following months, product sales did not return. Correlation analysis shows a strong negative relationship between price and sessions, page views and conversion rates. Their relevancy suffered directly from the increase in price.

We began working with this client in late August. They had ordered a thousand units of inventory after their initial success and were now stuck with a product that wasn't moving. We overhauled the product to create an optimized Amazon listing. Low relevancy keywords were removed. Then we began testing new pricing points to see how the product performed. As the product crossed the $10 per unit threshold there was a massive up-tick in conversion rates, orders and page views:

The inventory began flying off the shelf and thus the product relevancy was confirmed in Amazon's eyes again. Conversion rates reached as high 50% and page views increased by ~700%. The client was achieving success similar to their initial launch. We attempted to increase the price slightly over time and these metrics began decreasing again. The correlation analysis again showed a strong negative relationship between price and conversion rates, orders and page views. The client had achieved page one visibility, but was doing it a reduced profit in exchange for higher volume. Dropping pricing can be a powerful, yet tricky tool to impact the Amazon product ranking algorithm.

What Does All That Mean?

Pricing will directly impact your visibility within the Amazon product ranking algorithm. More importantly, **it shows that you need to differentiate your product**. This client was in a highly competitive market with a product that was just like everything else on the market. The private labeled item had no unique value proposition to customers and could only compete on price. We're now working with the client to improve their offering and achieve higher profits in the future.

Anyone could implement these same strategies to begin dominating a market. Downward pricing pressure from competitors will kill your product on Amazon. When choosing a product to sell, look for opportunities to differentiate yourself through bundling with a complimentary product or possibly working with your manufacturers to design unique features. Amazon is a great sales channel, but it's also extremely important to grow your product outside of the Amazon platform.

Utilize effective pricing on Amazon to get your product moving initially. Be willing to break even on your sales for as long as possible to develop the sales history that you need. Having a high-quality product and high volume of sales will lead to increased product reviews (or social proof) that will highlight your quality in shoppers' eyes. Do not drastically increase price to prevent selling out your inventory. This will kill your listing's relevancy within the Amazon product ranking algorithm. Slowly test increased pricing over time and check the sales data to see the impact it has on your listing. A differentiated product that has a unique value proposition to a client will be able to be priced higher without product relevancy being impacted as drastically.

7 Tips to Increase Your Amazon Sales

The question posed by many Amazon sellers is how to increase sales on the Amazon marketplace. Amazon is the largest and fastest growing ecommerce platform today and poses incredible opportunities for established businesses and startups. As opposed to search engines such as Google and Bing, Amazon users are potential customers looking to buy. The key to success on the platform is product visibility. This can be achieved in a few different ways. We've developed these ideas for selling on Amazon through our extensive client work. Check out our tips and tricks for selling on Amazon to learn how!

1. **Listing Optimization:** The Amazon search algorithm is designed to show customers the most relevant listings to their queries. It bases the relevancy on the keywords used throughout your product listing. Boosting sales on Amazon starts with the copywriting in your front end. It's important for two reasons: keyword relevancy; and, converting customers. Amazon crawls your listing's title, bullet points and product description for keywords and partly uses these to index your listing. It's important to have keyword rich content – but avoid keyword stuffing as the algorithm will recognize too much density as an attempt to manipulate the algorithm. This is against the TOS. Your listing also must convert page visitors so it's important to call out the features that make your product beneficial. Use the bullet points to highlight features and increase conversion rates.

2. **Backend Optimization:** It is also important to optimize the backend of your listing. The more information you provide to Amazon will help you index for the product better. One area

to utilize fully is the search term area. Amazon currently allows 1000 characters (including spaces) in each search term field. Use phrases and long tail keywords that customers could be searching for to find your product. To test if you are indexed for the search terms, copy and paste any random section. Search in Amazon and you should see your product come up within 24 hours.

3. **Advertising Campaigns:** Utilizing Amazon Sponsored Ads as a seller is an important part of how to increase sales on the Amazon marketplace. Showing up on page one is the goal of every seller. While it can happen right off the bat, chances are your product will not appear on the top pages. Running advertising campaigns is key to boosting sales on Amazon and moving up the search results pages. Run automatic campaigns to collect keyword ideas to use in your campaigns. Collect the data over a few weeks. Use the data from the reports to improve your backend search terms, listing page and build manual advertising campaigns. Bid higher on the manual advertising campaigns and let low bid automatic campaigns capture sales from keywords you may have missed. This can help you increase Amazon sales rank of your product by placing your product on the first page in the form of an advertisement.

4. **Product Promotions:** Utilizing the product promotions and giveaways features of seller central are great ideas for selling on Amazon. Enticing sellers to purchase your product through a discount can get you the momentum you need for boosting sales on Amazon. Amazon changed their review policy preventing sellers from providing discounts in exchange for reviews. Many sellers believe these reviews are how to increase sales on the Amazon marketplace. While reviews are important, the sales from these discounted purchases is what will increase Amazon sales rank and product visibility. You can publish discount codes directly on your listing or create a

promo codes that can be used in offsite marketing campaigns.

5. **Off-Platform Advertising:** One of the most important, yet least used tips and tricks is to advertise outside of the Amazon platform. Running social media ads can be a great way to build buzz for your product and generate sales. Utilize promotional codes to entice potential customers to learn more. Direct customers to a landing page where they can put in their email and receive the promo code. This allows you to build a customer list for future marketing and a better audience for your online advertising campaigns. This is how to increase sales on the Amazon marketplace in a major way!

6. **Selling Internationally:** Moving into international Amazon markets is another great way how to increase sales on the Amazon marketplace. The biggest markets outside of the US currently are Canada, the UK and Germany. The sales volume is smaller in these countries; however, the competition is also very low. Getting into a market early can position your product for long term sales. Utilizing Fulfillment by Amazon is the same as in the US. Each market has different tax requirements that you will need to consider. Soon you will be asking how to increase sales on Amazon UK!

7. **Product Price Point:** The price point of your product could be holding you back. Amazon tends to feature lower priced products toward the top of their pages. We've seen what simply dropping the price can do for boosting sales on Amazon. A recent client of ours dropped their price and went from no visibility to the 2nd page. The lower price will increase Amazon sales rank through additional sales. This can help you move up the rankings in extremely competitive markets. Make sure you have enough inventory before dropping the price too much or you could run out quickly!

This has only been a brief overview on how you can increase your Amazon sales. We've tested these ideas and many others with the clients we have worked with and seen incredible success. We believe that implementing these steps will help you increase your sales and improve your best seller ranking.

Leveraging Facebook Ads for Amazon Listings

Facebook ads is one of the channels that holds great promise for increasing conversions. Facebook is the biggest and fastest growing social media platform in the world. No other social media network can compare to its features, and most of all, its audience. Facebook has 1.86 billion monthly active users as of the fourth quarter of 2016. This is billions of potential customers for anyone with something to sell on Amazon. Facebook advertising is in constant revision, and it has grown to provide a wide array of features for advertisers. Sellers know that there will never be enough marketing channels, and Facebook ads is not one to miss.

Facebook Ads Capabilities

Facebook ads allows advertisers to target specific audiences and market products and services to them easily and effectively. Many sellers from Amazon FBA eCommerce retailers to big brands have been using Facebook ads to drive record sales and grow their businesses. Facebook has proven time and again to produce a very high ROI for many sellers. Some sellers have been so successful marketing with Facebook ads that they have recovered their ad spend by as much as 700%. Well-optimized campaigns have brought in so many new customers that Facebook has come to account for as much as 70% of sales for some businesses.

Facebook Ad Targeting

Facebook has exceptionally accurate targeting capabilities. The company has developed this mechanism over the years through data collection, analysis and improvements on their algorithms. By efficiently targeting billions of global users, Facebook presents a very attractive ad package. Through Facebook ads, sellers can identify and target specific audience segments for different products or for the same products at different times.

Ease of Use

The Facebook ad platform has been designed to be very easy to use. Even sellers with not a lot of experience on the platform or with ads themselves can navigate their ad accounts with relative ease. There are also many help resources available to provide support for getting started with audience searches and ad campaigns.

Organic Amazon Boost

Facebook is extremely effective at increasing sales. Amazon sellers can therefore experience organic ranking boosts for listings that receive traffic from Facebook ads. Organic rankings on Amazon are strictly monitored, so a true organic boost for any product is priceless. Sellers who direct traffic through ads with a good conversion rate will gain a valuable edge over the competition in the long run.

Getting Started

To begin using Facebook ads to boost your business sales, you will need to set up a business page and an ad account. Below we outline the simple steps that you will need to go through to prepare for your first Facebook ad campaign.

Your Facebook Business Page

1. Go to your Facebook Business account and click on the drop-down at the top right corner. Click on Create a Page.

2. From the available options, select the page category that best suits your business. Brand or Product is often the best choice

for Amazon sellers.

3. Next, select your industry-specific category, and enter your basic business information in the spaces provided.

4. Review your selection and entries and Agree to Facebook Pages terms and conditions when you are satisfied.

5. Click Get Started to launch your new business page.

6. Optimize your page by adding a concise and interesting description of your brand, a link to your Amazon page or your eCommerce website, and your logo as your profile picture.

7. Selest the option to reach more people to get more visitors to look at your page.

Your Facebook Ad Account

1. Open the Facebook Ads Manager and navigate to the Settings on the left side of the page.

2. Enter an account name, your business time zone, and your industry.

3. Select the option for using Facebook ads for business.

4. Carefully enter the additional required business information, review and finish.

5. Upload your product catalog to your account, including product names, images, pricing and other product details.

Install Conversion Tracking Pixel

The pixel is a code snippet that enables you to track visits, conversions and ROI from your Facebook ad account. The pixel also enables Facebook to use the tracking data to optimize your campaigns and build lookalike audiences to help you target better.

Once you have uploaded your catalog to your Business account, make sure that you add a custom audience pixel and set it to give you reports on your customers' buying behavior. This will help you identify site visitors for retargeting. Facebook needs time to gather data, so consider running your first ad campaign at least one month after your pixel is set up.

Lookalike Audiences

Facebook can use the data it has collected to help you to find new customers as well. Based on the demographics, characteristics and interests of past customers, Facebook can suggest Lookalike Audiences that you can advertise to. These audiences will have similar characteristics and therefore likely be interested in your products. Lookalike Audiences are a very high performing target group.

To create a Lookalike Audience, you first need a Custom Audience. You can build one from your Facebook Fans or data from your pixel.

Facebook Ad Types

Facebook ads in general are known to do wonders to increase traffic and conversions. There are, however, certain ad types that have proven more effective. Below we introduce the features of these Facebook ads to give you an overview of what you can expect.

Dynamic Product Ads

Dynamic product ads are possibly the highest ROI strategy. They are useful for regaining the interest of customers who are on the fence. These tailored Facebook ads can be targeted to specific customers based on their previous activity on your site. Amazon itself along with other eCommerce sites use Facebook retargeting to offer site visitors discounts and other enticements for recently viewed products.

Dynamic Product Ads feature prepared templates that pull the product names, images, pricing and other information straight from your product catalog. Whatever product details you have uploaded to Facebook Business Manager will be automatically reflected on the ad. This is especially useful for sellers with many products to manage.

All you need to launch a Dynamic Facebook ad is an ad title, your product names from the catalog, and keywords to find the right images. Then choose if you want to advertise products from your entire catalog or only specific categories. You can also display single or multi-product ads to your site visitors, regardless of what stage they reached.

Multi-Product Ads

Multi-product ads show multiple products to your audience in a single ad. This provides options for customers that you feel have not clicked buy or processed their carts because they are still looking around. With more choices, they are more likely to find what they want and complete their purchase. Multi-product ads can also be used to present the different features of one product or to test images for your listing by monitoring your click-through-rate. Cost per click also decreases over time as more people engage with the ads.

When using Multi-product ads separately from Dynamic Facebook campaigns, navigate to the Power Editor to begin setting up a standalone ad.

Run General Retargeting Campaigns

Abandoned carts is a huge eCommerce problem. As many as 70% of your customers may fail to complete their purchases. In addition, only 8% of them are likely to some back later. When you properly retarget these shoppers, you can encourage as many as 26% of them to come back to complete their orders. Retargeted ads in general have a click-through-rate that is ten times higher than regular ads.

To start running retargeting campaigns, navigate to the Power Editor to set up audiences and design your offers, upload coupons, or create single and multi-product ads.

Bonus Features

You can also use a series of Facebook ads to tell your brand story and to connect and build relationship with prospective and current customers. Short videos with a valuable message also communicate well and are well received even by people with limited time. With Custom Audiences, you can also create unique lists of people from emails or phone numbers. This way, you can reach out to your customers and encourage them to become your Facebook fans. Keep in mind that those customers who are great at sharing your posts should be rewarded with special offers and other perks.

Finding the Target Audience for Your Amazon Products with Facebook Ads

Utilizing Facebook ads to drive traffic to your Shopify store or Amazon listings is a powerful way to increase your products sales. The key to a successful, or cost effective, Facebook advertising campaign is to find your target audience – the consumers most likely to purchase your product. Running broad Facebook advertising campaigns will lead to higher cost per click (CPC) and will reach too many people who will never actually purchase your product. We're going to discuss ways to find the target audience for your Amazon products and how to refine that audience to maximize the return on investment from your advertising campaigns.

How to use Facebook Audience Insights to Your Advantage

Every Facebook Ads account has the Audience Insights page that is a powerful way to find the target audience for your Amazon products. You can look at audiences by location, age, gender and interests among many other factors. As you filter down through those factors, Audience insights will provide demographic information, the pages the like, their locations, online activity and purchasing behavior. We can use this information to begin creating a target audience for our products.

This is a great place to begin identifying your target audience. You will need to continually refine the audience by utilizing the Facebook Pixel. The pixel is installed on a landing page or in your Shopify store to gather information on the shoppers that click-through your advertisements on Facebook. You cannot, however, use a pixel if your ad is direct linking to your Amazon listings. Therefore, we recommend using a landing page service like ClickFunnels or AMZ Promoter if your goal is to increase sales on Amazon. Both services allow you to integrate the Facebook Pixel with your landing page.

2 Ways to Find the Target Audience for Your Amazon Products

The first step in finding your target audience will be to begin searching by interests. For this example, we will assume we are selling a camping product to illustrate how we choose the audience more effectively. We will search "Camping" in the interest field and check out the size of the overall audience. Audience Insights say that this interest has 10-15 million monthly active people on Facebook, which is a large audience. We are going to refine this audience down, but we typically want interest audiences that have 250,000+ monthly active users.

Next, we are going to look at the top 10 "Page Likes" for people in this interest category. We want to see how related the top page likes are to camping. Click through each page that comes up in the Top Categories section to see what these pages are related too. We typically look for about 80% or more of the pages to be related to camping. After we go through that, we are going to repeat that process by typing each page into the "Interests" search by itself to see how related those audiences are to camping. Not all pages will come up which typically means their audience is too small and Facebook does not have enough data on them. Exclude those pages from our list. Spend a good amount of time identifying pages and products that are related to your product.

Now we are going to break these pages into a few segments so that we can begin testing what segment has the best conversion rate. There are 4 main segments we look at. The first would be influencers or personas associated with the interest. These typically have dedicated fan bases that may be passionate about the product category. Next, we would look for information websites or pages that provide help or tips in this category. These audiences are actively seeking information on how to do or use something so there is a strong likelihood that they currently consume similar or related products. We are then going to look at publications or magazine pages, particularly those that have subscription services. People interested in these pages may own subscriptions to the publication and therefore have already purchased something in this category. Finally, we are going to look for product, program or service pages related to the interests. Like the prior category, these people have a higher likelihood of buying something in this category.

Set up the split test by creating 4 ad sets under 1 campaign – with each ad set focused on one of segments. We recommend setting a small daily budget of $5 or so per ad set so you do not blow through money. Install the Facebook pixel into your landing page to track the click-thru rate. You may see positive results that point to one segment being better than the others in as soon as 1 day.

Another way to identify the target audience will be through cross-referencing, or flex-targeting, pages and targeting high affinity pages. What do we mean by this? Facebook Ads give you the ability to refine audiences by page like. So, to cross-reference a camping interest we may enter the "Camping" interest into an ad and find an audience who likes camping and likes a related camping page we are cross-referencing it with. This leads to smaller, more targeted audiences. We split test that against the page affinities. Audience Insights also provides data on page affinities, which means the likelihood that the audience is going to engage with the content. Targeting high affinity pages can target people that are very interested in the category, and may also get us some free advertising if they share or like your content.

Take the list of pages that you have already researched and find their monthly audience numbers and affinity scores on the "Page Likes" section of Audience insights. Create a campaign and then create an ad set that we can use the cross-reference strategy on. Type in the main category interest into the "Detailed Targeting" section, so in this case Camping. Below that field, you will notice a link to "Narrow Audience" appears. Select it, and then begin typing in an interest to see how it affects the audience size. The goal is to get an audience size between about 75,000-500,000. You can do that by entering multiple requirements into the first "Narrow Audience" field – or by adding additional cross-references by selecting "Narrow Further." Once we reach the ideal audience size, we will have a very focused audience to begin split testing with.

We will begin split testing the audience in the above paragraph against an audience of high affinity pages. Look at the list of page affinities and find what the average affinity is. Take those pages with the above average affinity scores for our comparison audience. We will then set up the campaign with two ad sets – one testing the cross-reference segment versus the affinity segment. Set the budgets for each segment at about $5 per day. Make sure your ad is going to a landing page with the Facebook Pixel installed to track your click-thru rates.

There is no easy way to track actual conversions if your traffic is being direct to Amazon. You are not able to install the Facebook Pixel onto page listings. One thing you could do to see conversions coming through Facebook ads would be to create a unique promo code for a small percentage off that you use exclusively to market your content in the Facebook ad. You can then go back through your orders and see what orders had this code applied. It won't be specific to which ad set got the sale, but as you begin narrowing by pausing ad sets you can gain a better idea by seeing if your conversions increase or decrease with each change.

It's important to find the target audience for your Amazon Products to increase your products sales. Directing traffic through Facebook to your listings can be a great way to build your sales history and boost the product up the page rankings. These two strategies have led to increased sales for our clients and can do the same for you. You can also implement these same audience targeting strategies to drive traffic to Shopify, BigCommerce or WooCommerce stores as well!

CREATING A SALES FUNNEL FOR AMAZON

Marketing campaigns through Amazon can drive additional traffic to your listings and hopefully increase conversions. A more powerful way to advertise your product on Amazon – or any ecommerce platform for that matter – would be to create a sales funnel. Being 100% reliant on the Amazon platform for sales is not a winning strategy and can set you up for hardship in the future. By creating a sales funnel for Amazon, you can find potentially interested customers to purchase your product and continue to target them in the future.

What is a Sales Funnel?

A sales funnel is what many ecommerce companies and service oriented companies use to attract potential customers and turn them into consumers. Many companies use the image of an upside-down pyramid separated into different parts to represent it. The top of the upside-down pyramid (essentially the base) is all your marketing efforts to find potential customers that may be interested in your product. As customers enter the funnel they are funneled into the middle of the pyramid where the sales process occurs. This is where the customer learns more about your product and decides if this is something that will make their life easier or better. Finally, at the bottom of the upside-down pyramid, you have your customers who decided to purchase.

Why are Sales Funnels Important?

Sales funnels are important as they provide a few different benefits to a seller. One of the benefits is that a sales funnel can be used to drive traffic to your listing. The depth of many of the categories on

Amazon can make it very difficult for your product to show up on search results pages, particularly in competitive markets. Utilizing a sales funnel strategy can be a great way to get your product in front of potential customers, start converting sales and move up the Amazon rankings organically.

Another great benefit of a sales funnel is building a target audience. A good sales funnel allows a seller to collect email addresses of their potential customers through an opt-in page. You can use these emails to create target audiences on many advertising platforms and find more potential customers. The emails can also be used in email marketing campaigns to let customers know of new products you may be rolling out, discounts you are offering or possibly to retarget them for the original product.

How to Create a Sales Funnel?

The most effective way to create a sales funnel is through utilizing social media advertising. Use social media platforms to market to potential customers and to grow your product or brand awareness. Make sure your advertisement has some benefit to the potential customer that will entice them to click. As potential customers begin to click on your advertisement they will need to be redirected to an email opt-in page. Many social media platforms will not allow you to link directly to Amazon and will need to go through a landing page or your website first. Once they opt-in to receive the benefit that was advertised to them, they can be redirected to learn more about the product or redirected to the Amazon page to purchase the product.

Utilizing Social Media Influencer Marketing

Influencer marketing is not at all a new marketing strategy, but the tactic has gained traction quite rapidly on social media in the last year or so. The words of those that the public has grown to love and respect go a long way in boosting recognition for products and services. And what better way to get those recommendations out today than via social channels? Savvy consumers tend to steer clear of advertising because they no longer trust these types of messages. A thumbs up from a renowned celebrity appearing in their feed, however, will be paid due attention.

Two things combine to make influencer marketing a powerhouse strategy. First, no form of advertising can yet compete with word of mouth. Second, social media is where everyone is at these days. This is why leveraging social media influencer marketing can increase brand awareness and raise conversion rates by as much as 50%. Once your influencer marketing campaign is off the ground, word is also likely to spread even further as other fans share the posted recommendations. That's free marketing right there, which can give your sales another boost. In 2016, social media influencer marketing became an established form of promotion. In 2017, it is set to blast through the roof with 50% of brands signifying intent to dive into influencer marketing campaigns.

Influencer Marketing Explained

Influencer marketing is a strategy that relies on the popularity and authority of a known figure in a certain industry. A social influencer is an authoritative figure who has gained standing in social circles. There are many such online celebrities who have gained a solid following and actively engage fans on different topics. They do not necessarily give full product endorsements or testimonials about specific services, but may work in mentions from time to time in their daily updates. Being an influencer is linked to a certain charisma, and people flock to such magnets and almost cling to their every word.

More than just gaining exposure, influencer marketing gets your product or service in front of targeted audiences and associated with the big names that will draw conversions. It isn't the type of direct advertising that has become such a huge turn off. It is the guy next door's favorite online talent just sharing his thoughts on this or that with everyone tuning in to see what he has to say. Consumer reviews have already proven to be a huge factor in purchasing decisions, and having an influencer leave a similar comment on any one of the many popular networks is a powerful thing.

Putting good money into influencer marketing may seem like a frivolous investment at first glance. Interests shift faster than the sands of the Sahara, and social media trends follow. Influencers know this, however, and so fiercely guard their audiences. They want to make sure that they never sell out because they know that as soon as they let their genuine voice slip away, their fans will quickly follow. They must keep the experience organic to survive, and brands can ride this trend for as long as the world appreciates authenticity.

Integrating Influencer Marketing

Influencer marketing is, simply put, finding the right pull for your push and investing in getting those mentions for your brand. You can get started on making it an integral part of your marketing with the following steps.

Set Goals Aligned with Your brand image and larger Strategy

Every successful brand has a closely guarded image and well-maintained message. Set your goals for your influencer marketing campaign so that they flow seamlessly with your content strategy and positively build your brand's reputation. Influencers can help boost product launches, generate hype for events, create and promote new content, and turn bad PR around. If you are working in any of these areas in your current strategy, you can begin your search for the right influencer to carry it out.

Identify and Locate Your Influencer

The best social influencer for your specific goals will have a sizable audience composed of the perfect set of individuals for your offerings and the level of credibility that you need to achieve your targets. Your influencer will have an authentic voice that supports your image and evidently attracts and keeps the attention of your target market. He or she will also have a consistent presence on the best channels for your desired audience. You will be able to see and feel how much trust the audience places in your prospective influencer, and gauge the potential impact from there.

To find such influencers, you will need to get on social networks and do an active search. There are a few types of software available that can make the search easier, but a manual search will allow you to follow leads that a machine would miss and to get a real feel of how your prospects move within their spheres of influence. Remember that influencer marketing revolves around word of mouth, so when you find one or two that you like, ask them to point out a few others who might work for your campaign as well.

Make Contact and Offer Value

When it is time to reach out to social influencers to form relationships, you should always make direct contact. Using an agency might take less of your time, but this is part of that old advertising system that influencers and their followers stay far away from. Get in touch directly to show your sincerity. Just as you would with a fresh sales lead, be honest and personable, avoiding the sales talk and focusing more on learning about them. From there, you can learn what drives them to do what they do, and be able to offer them real value in exchange for their help.

Keep Track of Progress

Influencer marketing falls within the realm of native advertising, but this organic approach can still be monitored. Even if you are just using a simple spreadsheet to take note of posts and updates about your brand and offerings, you can keep an eye on what is happening and how it is helping you reach the goals that you have set.

Take It a Step Further

Once you have formed stable relationships with key influencers, you can level-up your influencer marketing campaign by inviting them to post on your social channels. This will firm up the connection between the authority and your brand. It will also help you gain more followers on your business accounts.

Act Fast!

Since influencer marketing is still a relatively open area as businesses continue to test the waters, you can make a big splash and net a good number of big fish for a small fee if you act quickly and start making influencer marketing part of your marketing strategy today. Influencer marketing is has not reached its saturation point yet, but marketers are catching on and companies will soon be competing for the best names to speak for their brands. Now is the time to get in the game and capture these powerful movers before they establish ties with the competition.

SEARCH ENGINE OPTIMIZATION FOR AMAZON MOBILE SHOPPERS

Mobile shopping is on the rise and is predicted to double in four short years. The problem is that the mobile experience is horribly lacking, particularly around optimization. Buyers spend 20% more-time shopping via mobile devices, but end up spending only a sixth of what they do on desktops. Many are abandoning their carts in frustration because mobile commerce should be more convenient, but just doesn't offer the same quality results. Sellers and brands who fail to create an optimized mobile shopping experience are losing as much as a 65% increase in sales.

The good news for Amazon vendors is that the fully optimized Amazon app is drawing these shoppers away from other stores who are unprepared to offer the best mobile experience. This means that the market is ready, but the question is whether vendors are set to receive the incoming flood of around half of all mobile shoppers. Many vendors have become quite adept at optimizing their listings for e-commerce desktop users, and it is now time to get started on perfecting these listings for m-commerce.

The Mobile Experience

One of the key elements in optimizing Amazon listing content for mobile users is consideration for the mobile experience. Basically, mobile devices have smaller screens, and mobile users have less time. These two main points affect m-commerce in very similar ways. For instance, it is tiresome to try to read through long descriptions on a mobile device, and mobile users are usually on the go, and cannot spare the extra few minutes that it would take to get through a listing to find what they are looking for. Because these users are normally busy doing something else while browsing, they are more likely to select a product that can show them the most important information upfront. An optimized m-commerce Amazon listing therefore presents clear and concise information that these users can easily accommodate.

Optimizing for Mobile

Keywords

Keywords are still a very important component of your m-commerce listing text. The Amazon App search feature uses them in much the same way as the desktop version does to identify the closest matching products. The trick here is to add your relevant keywords in a shorter format. It may be tempting to use all the available characters, but this can dilute your content and bore your typical mobile shopper.

You should look for a balance here:

1. Focus on the main key words and phrases that rank the highest for searches.

2. Incorporate another one or two in a straightforward description of your product's main benefits.

3. Incorporate another one or two in your best use cases.

4. Incorporate another one or two in your best examples.

5. Incorporate one or two in a tagline, or a summarized version of your brand mission.

This is a basic suggestion, but you should feel free to play around with the text to get the most coherent and complete whole. The elements can be combined in your five sentences as you see fit to aid in emphasizing your product's best features and strongest selling points.

Titles

Your product titles will render differently on mobile than they do on desktop. Most often, titles will be shortened to save space, so you will need to arrange your titles so that the most important words are at the beginning. These can be your best keywords, or your brand name if it is a popularly searched term. Coherence is better than cramming, so you should develop short phrases of four words on average and separate these with commas so that readers won't get confused.

Writing Copy

Once you have your sentences with keywords, it is important to check for readability. Pay close attention to the proper placement of these keywords so that they aid comprehension rather than cloud it. Next, make sure that the text flows together nicely from one point to the next so that they can get all the information effortlessly. You want them to be able to skim through at least this first and most essential part of your listing. If the text is disorganized or distracting, mobile users will rarely take a second look to understand it better, and will leave without the great takeaway that will hook them into buying from you.

Formatting Text

There are two main sections in an Amazon listing, the Features and Details and the Product Description. The first section is where you should separate your five content elements above into bullet points. This makes it easier for the mobile reader to take in small chunks of information at a time, facilitating faster comprehension. Bolding, italicizing, and using all caps for the most important words and phrases further enhances your customers' experience.

The Description will most often not be read by mobile shoppers. However, if you could capture their attention above, they may decide to read on. This usually means that they are serious about making a purchase. To keep them keen on your product, it is best to use the same formatting strategy in your Description so that readers can still skim through to pick up the salient points. Since this section will have much longer text than above, use line breaks to separate your paragraphs. This works in the same way as using bullet points in the above. Saving one format type, such as all caps, for prefacing points will also help mobile users to absorb your content more easily to keep them interested for the close.

Tips & Tricks for Selling Internationally with Amazon

Making the decision to begin selling internationally can be daunting. Enthusiasm can be dampened by the anxiety that often goes along with the prospect of going global. Sellers must weigh various considerations before launching a global expansion. Accurate timing for the move is essential to getting good results faster, and rolling out to the global market with a full appreciation of the risks and costs is crucial to business success.

The Right Time to Go Global

If you have been thinking about whether you should start offering your brands and products to overseas markets, one or more of the following situations may have prompted you to start planning:

- Stagnant or scant growth in your current market and the need to reach additional markets to meet sales targets; or, great success in your current market, suggesting that it makes sense to move to the next level

- The promise of increased profits based on advantageous logistics in markets closer to the manufacturing source

- Inquiries from shoppers located outside your current market, indicating or supporting an impression that your brands and products would fill a need and be in high demand in other markets

Every business must be able to adapt to the market and seize opportunities for growth. With Amazon, the marketplace is no longer limited to Amazon.com and its linked markets in Canada and Mexico. Amazon

Europe offers five additional sites that can service a very large market comprised of nearly thirty countries in the European Union, and Amazon Asia offers three sites in the key countries of Japan, China and India that are poised to take the continent by storm in the next few years.

Amazon has strategically expanded to make selling internationally more attractive. They have taken advantage of the international markets that hold the top eCommerce promise. Joining Amazon at these hot global spots grants you entry to millions of new potential customers without having to start from scratch with the additional investments normally associated with a new location. Moreover, you can begin enjoying immediate returns because Amazon has already built trust with these shoppers.

Recognizing the Challenges

Having an amazing marketplace laid out before you is tempting; however, there are still several concerns involved in global expansion. Below are some of these considerations that must be carefully contemplated before delving into selling internationally.

Marketing Challenges

- Creating local awareness, such as starting fresh with no reviews

- Pricing adjustments to compensate for different costs and market tolerance

- Import restrictions

- Promotional timing, knowledge of local exposure points

- Product variety

Merchandising Challenges

- Changes in packaging and completing product information for compliance

- Compliance with regulations (both US and new market) such as privacy and security

Business and Financial Challenges

- Creating a local entity

- Credit-card fraud

- Additional costs for compliance testing, and for taxes, duties and customs fees

- Currency conversions, local banking and credit card processing

Operational Challenges

- Updating SKUs and translating listings for compliance

- Logistics issues such as shipping delays and fulfillment options

- Package inclusions

Customer Service Challenges

- Language barrier

- Customer service hours

- Managing returns

Technology Challenges

- Updating checkout fields and calculating additional fees

- Multicurrency pricing and multilingual views

Tips on Selling Internationally

Going global with your brands and products is a long-term commitment that will require a certain level of energy and financial support.

1. ***Quantify your Marketing Resources*** – Do you have what it takes to back up your global expansion over a period of three, five, or even ten years?

2. ***Commit to the Long-Term Process of Going Global*** – Are you prepared to begin the process of properly marketing your products to and streamlining your service process for a new market? Do you have substantial knowledge of the market to adjust your expectations and generate significant demand?

3. ***Get to Know the Culture*** – Are you familiar with different aspects of the buying culture, such as payment preferences?

4. ***Research Your Sales Channels*** – What have you learned about the general eCommerce atmosphere in your proposed new target market? Are you familiar with options within that area that are outside of Amazon?

5. ***Familiarize Yourself with Additional Duties, Taxes, Import Fees and Customs Brokerage*** – Do you know how to compute for customs fees? Are you familiar with VAT? Are you aware of the associated penalties for non-compliance? Do you know what you need to get your EORI? Is your accountant prepared to handle sales in different international jurisdictions?

6. ***Lay out a Plan for Logistics Changes*** – Do you have a plan in place for handling warehousing? Returns? Additional shipping stops for FBA preparation?

This list is by no means exhaustive, but a sampling of the different obstacles that you must prepare for before you can start safely selling internationally on the Amazon marketplace, or on other channels. Take the time to go through all the different nuances of selling in each of your prospective marketplaces. You may find that some of the locations that you wanted to enter look more manageable or more profitable than at first glance. If you have taken in all that needs to be done for a successful entry as an international seller, have all the resources to do what it takes, and are still excited about launching an expansion, then the time is right for you to start selling internationally.

Selling on Amazon's Other Websites

Selling on Amazon is rewarding enough, but it became more enticing when Amazon acquired the very popular daily deal site Woot in 2010. This is not the only subsidiary that they own, however. The top destination for online shoppers is not called the online retail giant for nothing. Below we have an overview of the biggest of the websites and companies under the Amazon banner: online retailers Shopbop and Zappos, self-publishing platform CreateSpace, video streaming service Twitch.tv, audio bookstore Audible, audio book publisher Brilliance Audio, rare bookstore AbeBooks, gaming studio Double Helix Games, and maritime forwarding business Beijing Century Joyo Courier Service. Selling on Amazon now has new meaning with these and other avenues for online retail.

Shopbop – 2006

This online retailer has expanded its services since it was acquired by Amazon. Already trusted with a global customer base, Shopbop continues to sell high quality authentic designer merchandise for women. The site boasts a wide range of hand-picked apparel and accessories from fashion's current labels. Shopbop is known for its superb personalized customer service, which includes wardrobe advice. The site also offers front-line editorial lookbooks and select partnerships with future-focused brands.

Zappos – 2009

This online retailer is one of the largest online shoe stores in the world. The idea behind the company was to build a website that offered a large, high quality assortment of shoes. Zappos now also offers the best selection of clothing, accessories, bags, boutique, and various other items for men, women and children. The Zappos goal is to give the best service online in any category with a focus on fast shipping. The continuing goal of Zappos is to get customers to associate the Zappos brand with the absolute best service.

CreateSpace – 2005

This self-publishing platform is the result of a merging of two companies that Amazon acquired in the same year, CustomFlix and Book-Surge. CreateSpace offers self-publishing to authors, independent filmmakers and musicians. Subscribers can publish their own original works and easily distribute them through an on-demand system. The company offers these independents an innovative way to market their work to a wide audience while maintaining a good deal of control over the material.

Twitch.tv – 2014

This live video streaming platform focuses on live streams. Most content consists of video gaming, including competitive gaming event coverage, playthroughs of video games, multiplayer gaming, and broadcasts of eSports competitions. Twitch boasts a subscriber base of 100 million monthly visitors who have access to video material from 1.5 million broadcasters.

Audible – 2008

This audio bookstore focuses on the production and sale of audio entertainment, but also deals in online educational and information programs. Audible stocks audiobooks, audio versions of magazines and newspapers, and radio and TV programs. Since the acquisition, Audible has assimilated about five thousand Audio GO titles. Possibly Amazon's most recognized subsidiary, Audible is the biggest name in audiobook production and retail in the United States.

Brilliance Audio – 2007

This company is the leading independent US audiobook publisher. Brilliance Audio maintains a very high standard of audiobook publishing. They were producing audio copies of bestselling books at affordable prices long before the term audiobook was coined. The company is in a great position to compete for top fiction and nonfiction works of all genres with their reputation and fully equipped manufacturing facilities, studios, art department and global sales team. Brilliance Audio pursues its motto of "Audiobooks for Everyone" with more than 6500 titles to date on CD, MP3-CD, and for download, and offers volume publishing for certain print publishers.

AbeBooks – 2008

This book company works with independent bookstores to track down rare, used and out-of-print books. They pride themselves in a sizeable inventory of rare titles made available in over fifty countries and from thousands of booksellers. AbeBooks has six websites for France, Germany, Italy, Spain, North America, and the United Kingdom.

Double Helix Games – 2014

This gaming studio, famous for the games "Killer Instinct" and "Silent Hill", has more than a hundred game developers working on new games. The company hosts frequent studio events and focuses on maintaining an atmosphere that is most conducive to creativity and excellence. Double Helix Games is the result of a merger of The Collective and Shiny Entertainment; both Foundation 9 studios. The company is now one of the largest and most experienced in game development worldwide. They are also one of the developers of major home consoles.

BONUS for Selling on Amazon: Beijing Century Joyo Courier Service – 2016

This maritime forwarding business is part of Amazon's major drive to expand their logistics strategy to sea freight. Amazon has begun posting its rates for this new service, ready to compete with experienced global freight companies in China. Amazon's application for a license was approved by the US Federal Maritime Commission in early 2016, and the company is now pushing forward with its plans to operate as a non-vessel operating common carrier (NVOCC). Beijing Century Joyo has already run 150 containers of cargo shipment to and from China and the US. This may bring additional benefits to selling on Amazon for Chinese manufacturers. As Chinese shippers take this more affordable and direct option, savings are likely to filter down and make selling on Amazon an even more lucrative business.

Selling on Amazon's Deal Site Woot

Aside from the Amazon marketplace in North America, Europe and Asia, this mega company holds several other subsidiaries. A few of these are eCommerce sites, and the biggest of these smaller companies include online retailers Shopbop and Zappos, self-publishing platform CreateSpace, video streaming service Twitch.tv, audio bookstore Audible, audio book publisher Brilliance Audio, rare bookstore AbeBooks, gaming studio Double Helix Games, and maritime forwarding business Beijing Century Joyo Courier Service. Perhaps the most notable of these subsidiaries is Woot, known as the original daily-deal site. Below, we give you an introduction to Woot's sales model, marketing style, and a guide to begin selling on the site.

The Woot Sales Model

Woot is an online retailer popular for its main theme of offering different discounted products every day. The company's tagline is, unsurprisingly, "One Day, One Deal". The main website originally offered only one discounted product each day. The item would never be announced in advance, but it was usually electronics or computer hardware. The item would sell until it was sold out, and the next item would generally not be offered until midnight. After being acquired by Amazon.com in 2010, Woot began offering a new item if the day's item sold out before noon.

Other Woot sites offer daily deals for t-shirts, children's items, wine, household goods, tools, fashion accessories, sports equipment and other various items. Only the t-shirts were originally shipped outside of the United States, with all other items sent courier for a fixed fee regardless of weight or size. Since the acquisition, Woot is tied into the Amazon distribution network. Some shipping delays are still experienced since some items that are sold are not actually in stock. Woot customers can grab a limited number of deal items, sometimes one and a maximum of three. Some Woot deals are on refurbished items, which has caused data leaks on at least one occasion.

The one-deal-a-day Woot business model means that replacements are not offered for defective products. Customers can only request refunds, and customer support is non-existent. Woot customers are referred to the manufacturer or the user community on the Woot forums to file complaints or get information.

The Woot Marketing Style

Woot is a fun site that leverages humor to sell products. Product descriptions are strange and even crazy, often mocking not only the product but also the customer and Woot itself. Descriptions also straightforwardly acknowledge product downsides. The serious details of the products are also available, however, below the Woot description. Advice from the Woot community is also readily available through the forums, which function much like Amazon reviews in guiding would-be buyers. The forum is kept lively by various contests that are more for enjoyment than prize value.

Woot Benefits

The self-proclaimed primary benefit of selling on Woot is their honed mechanism for running flash deals. As the website Vendor FAQ explains, they are a good way to dispose of excess inventory, even items that would seem difficult to sell off. Woot agrees to take item quantities upfront, and pays vendors when the orders for the deal items have shipped out.

Woot will also take practically any kind of item. Vendors are welcome to send in their best offers to be evaluated by the team, who will then offer suggestions and a customized plan to suit vendor needs, such as disposing of unwanted items or testing the salability of a new product. Woot also offers several deal formats, such as featured daily deals, extended flash sales and the classic Woot-off sale that can extend the daily deal for a certain item to three days.

Vendors can take advantage of the Woot community as well as the sales members who often post detailed information about certain products and which features make them sell better. The marketing model is also a unique and powerful attraction factor.

Selling on Woot

To start selling on Woot, there is an onboarding process that is similar to becoming a vendor on Amazon. Prospective vendors will need to agree to the shipping and vendor terms, and submit a W9 to their assigned vendor manager. Successfully onboarded vendors can then start submitting deals and can expect to launch a deal within a month from that date.

Woot vendors will need to go through the SellerCloud integration process, which includes manual order import and tracking export. Vendors who have integrated a website that is not on the Magento platform will need to create a separate company for Woot orders to distinguish them from other orders made on the website. Inventory is not updated from SellerCloud with inventory feeds, however, so creating shadows is not necessary.

Plugins are available to facilitate the process. These plugins are placed on the vendor's server. Note that files must be imported manually since Woot does not support FTP access. Vendors can customize plugins to suit their needs, but different rates may apply for these changes. SellerCloud Support can provide details on the available plugin versions and customizations.

Order Imports

The SellerCloud Support plugin to take care of order import permits the direct import of Woot generated files. Customization includes importing orders as wholesale. To import an order, go to Import Orders under the Order menu and choose the company you want to transact with. Choose the option to use Website as the Channel and choose the Woot plugin from the dropdown. Select the order file that you want to upload from your computer and press the Import button.

Tracking Export

To export Woot-ready shipping confirmations, you can use the tracking export plugin. Go to Manage Orders and select the orders in question. Go to the action Menu and choose Export Orders, then press Go or the export icon located at the top right of the grid. Choose the Woot tracking export plugin and click the Export button. The task will be queued and the download will be available once completed, ready for upload to Woot. Shipped Woot orders can also be scheduled to export, along with other recurring tasks.

5 Steps to Drive More Traffic to Your Shopify Store

Creating a successful ecommerce presence involves utilizing as many platforms as possible to reach your audience. Shopify is a great platform to expand your brand's online presence and bring in additional revenue to your business. We are going to cover ways to drive more traffic to your Shopify store.

The three ways we are going to drive traffic will be through search engine optimization (SEO), social media marketing and affiliate marketing. These play an important role in attracting more shoppers to your website. Following these strategies will set your Shopify store – and your brand – up for long term eCommerce success. It all begins by increasing your online presence!

Increase Your Social Media Presence

Reaching your target audience is simpler than ever thanks to the innumerable social media networks that exist. Your brand needs to have as large a social media presence as possible. It's important to be on the top social media sites for two reasons. Creating social media profiles gives you the opportunity to create links to your Shopify store – which is a huge part of SEO. It is known as link building. The Google search engine indexes your website based on a variety of factors and one of them is the quality of your links. It is important to have links back to your website from "quality" websites. The idea is to get as many links from places like Facebook, Twitter, YouTube, etc. directing people to your website.

Having social media presence on a variety of websites will continue to pay dividends down the road. It will allow you to reach a larger audience and can snowball into additional backlinking to your website. A strong social media presence in combination with the steps below are key as you try to drive more traffic to your Shopify store.

Utilize Facebook Advertising to Better Understand Your Audience

Gaining insight to who your target audience is will be valuable. Facebook advertising provides a great opportunity to collect demographic information on who clicks on your links. Facebook tracks the behaviors and interests of their users. You can obtain that information by creating campaigns on the platform. Facebook ads can be used in a couple different ways. The easiest way to collect the information is to install a Facebook pixel into your Shopify store and create ads directly linking to your website. A Facebook pixel can be used to track different metrics you may be interested in – from page views to conversions. Having a pixel on your website will collect the demographic information as customers visit your site.

Another way you can use Facebook ads is to redirect potential customers to a landing page – either a Facebook landing page or an off-site landing page. The landing page needs to have some type of value proposition to attract shoppers. The value proposition could be a discount or a free eBook on a topic that the shopper gets after entering their email address. Email address collection is the primary goal of using a landing page. The email addresses can be used for advertising campaigns or for email marketing campaigns in the future.

You will be able to collect the demographic information from either method. This demographic information will allow you to create "look-a-like" audiences in the future. This means that the customers you target on Facebook will have similar behaviors and interests to those who previously clicked on your advertisements. You will also use this demographic information in the next 3 steps as well to drive more traffic to your Shopify store.

Design and Create Content for Your Audience

The demographic data from Facebook will provide great insight to who your audience is. It will provide detailed info on ages, sex, location, interests and behaviors. Your job is to create content that people in those demographics will be interested in. For example, a target audience of 30-49 interested in home appliances may not care much about appliances in new rental units. That audience is typically going to be homeowners and content centered on that topic may not be important to them. On the other hand, content about the top, new appliances that will increase the value of their home could be hugely relevant.

Each audience will be different and you will need to design your content around your audience. Create content that adds value to your target audience and will keep them coming back for more. It's not the quantity of content you put out, but how relevant and valuable it is to your audience. Use the social media profiles you created to distribute the content you create. Install a blog on your Shopify store and post the content there. Ensure the content always has links to your website and other relevant websites. As the content is liked and shared by your audience, more traffic will reach your website and, for SEO purposes, the links to your store will greatly increase.

Content marketing can be a great way to drive more traffic to your Shopify store. It will also be valuable in the next step.

Using Affiliate Marketing Programs to Increase Sales

Creating or enrolling your product in an affiliate marketing program can be a powerful way to get more sales on your Shopify store and increase brand awareness. Affiliate marketing is where you provide commissions for other people to sell your products. Many marketers make their entire living off affiliate marketing and are professionals at what they do. They utilize a variety of techniques like social media marketing, search engine marketing, email marketing and content marketing to reach potential customers. Each affiliate has their own link which records sales that their advertisements get you. You pay them a commission on each sale that they get you. Many times, the content that you have created can also be used by – or improved by – affiliates to drive more traffic to your Shopify store.

Utilizing affiliate marketing may not be for everyone. There are 3 important factors to consider when deciding whether to use affiliate marketers. The first is if your product's pricing allows for enticing commissions for the affiliates. A 50% commission on a $10 product is certainly not as enticing for a 50% commission on a $50 product. The second is if you have the margins to pay an enticing commission. Shopify may allow you to price your products higher than the Amazon platform, but if you're costs are too high you may not make much or any profit from affiliate sales. This is not necessarily a bad thing however. Breaking even on an affiliate sale could make it worthwhile for you. The content they create may increase your brand awareness, drive additional traffic and increases links to your website. It can also increase customer retention for products that may be consumable. The final factor to consider is whether you have inventory or manufac-turing capabilities to keep up with the increased sales from affiliates. Running out of inventory costs affiliates money as their advertise-ments may still be running. This may turn off potential affiliates from working with you.

Utilizing Influencer Marketing to Drive More Traffic to Your Shopify Store

The final step in driving traffic to your website is by reaching out to influencers. Reaching out to topic experts is a great way to get your product more visibility. Experts run blogs, podcasts or social media accounts with large followings. You may be able to get your prod-uct featured on their outlet by either sponsoring them, offering the product to them for free or guest blogging for them (great for SEO!). Each expert and what they may be looking for will be different. Trying reaching out to as many as possible to see if there are any opportunities available.

Social media influencers typically have massive followings that are interested in a topic. They typically use the Instagram, Twitter, Facebook or Snapchat platforms to reach people. You can propose having your product featured on their feed when you reach out to them. Influencers will charge you a fee to have the product featured for a certain amount of time, but the fee can be reasonable. In our experience, Instagram is typically where you will find the most reasonable fees. It is important to see what their engagement is relative to their followers. Many pages will buy followers to artificially inflate that number. There are almost unlimited interest pages on Instagram so shop around and find a deal that is right for you.

These 5 steps to drive more traffic to your Shopify store will product incredible results. Some of our clients' stores have been able to achieve over $100,000 in monthly revenue. Growing your brand outside the Amazon platform is key for your long-term success. There are incredible ecommerce opportunities available to those who are willing to put in the work.

Resources

Shopify
One of the fastest growing and most popular eCommerce store front website hosting programs that can be integrated with Amazon accounts to allow customers quick purchases
www.shopify.com

Maximizing Your Google Shopping Sales Channel

Google Shopping has a lot to offer online businesses. Some optimization is needed, however, for the platform to be effective. If you want to take advantage of this opportunity for growth, read on to learn about structuring campaigns and adjusting your shopping feed. Google Shopping can be a boon to your eCommerce store if you can invest some time into getting it set up to maximize potential revenue.
Mobile Influence

The world's shoppers are using mobile more and more. Over half off all Google Shopping clicks are from mobile devices. Just two years ago, mobile only accounted for about 20% of all clicks on the platform. It is due to this rapid increase in shopping click volume that Google Shopping ads are now filling the top half of the first page of Google's search engine results on mobile devices. Organic rankings and text ads are no longer visible.

To make the most of your Google Shopping campaigns, you need to keep abreast of these mobile trends. If you are getting half of your hits from mobile shoppers, then you need to do all that you can to ensure the success of your mobile campaigns rather than leaving mobile conversions to chance. Because of the very high volume of mobile traffic that we are seeing in general, and the continuing upward trend over the past two years, mobile is the future.

It is necessary for businesses to create both a mobile and a desktop strategy - possibly with a heavier focus on mobile advertising campaigns going forward. This thrust will require that you tweak the default settings in Google Shopping. The recommended settings are not going to get you anywhere near the level of profits that you could be raking in if you were to customize your campaigns.

Separate Mobile Campaigns

Because mobile shopping covered such a small margin until the massive surge between 2015 and 2016, most businesses did not bother to use the mobile targeting options that were available. Now, however, ignoring this market would be a grave error in judgment. Fortunately, AdWords is undergoing an overhaul. At first, there was no way to set Google Shopping campaigns to target different device types. Businesses could still tweak settings specifically for mobile to adjust bids and fine-tune ad settings, but the options are limited. Upcoming changes due to launch this year will make mobile targeting for each campaign even better with specific settings for desktop, tablets, and mobiles.

Mobile campaigns used to consist of dummy bids based on the desktop campaigns, which were simply a certain percentage of the desktop bids. This was the only way that the platform would be able to distinguish whether each click was for desktop or for mobile traffic. Google Shopping will soon allow businesses to create separate campaigns that give business owners complete control over all aspects of a campaign.

For advertising strategies that warrant separate campaigns to properly target desktop versus mobile users, this is great news. Business owners should be aware, however, that not all businesses need to make the additional investment to manage separate mobile and desktop strategies. The option is there, however, to use when a business sees a significant increase in mobile traffic.

Campaign Structure

The way that you structure your campaigns is going to have a big impact on how they perform. Take advantage of the different options that you have on Google Shopping to optimize your audience targeting, bids and feed. This way, you will be able to spend less and get better results faster.

Geographic and Demographic Targeting

A few tweaks for geographic and demographic targeting can refine your campaigns to make sure that your ad investment is well spent. The early stages of your campaigns are the research phase, when you should be gathering a lot of data so you can use it to make good decisions regarding your campaigns.

The Google Shopping default location is the entire United States. While this may seem like a good way to reach a wider audience, it is impractical. Businesses will usually get much more hits from certain states as compared to others. Targeting the whole country does not make good business sense. By learning which areas are bringing in the highest conversions, you can refine your geographic targeting and see an immediate increase in your ROI.

Demographic targeting options are not available by default on Google Shopping, so business owners must manually turn them on. To test the waters, you can add target groups to a campaign without setting bids and allow them to collect information before you begin spending on ads. You can also take advantage of demographic targeting to see even more data on who is showing interest in a product and who is buying it. You can also check socio-economic levels to see which areas have the extra income that makes shoppers more likely to seriously consider purchasing your products.

Custom Labels

Without custom labels, you will not be able to segment your ads to target different groups for specific products. Once you have collected a significant amount of information on your ideal audience, you will want to streamline your campaigns. You can save a lot of ad capital and put it to better use by serving ads for different products only to those who are most likely to be interested in and able to make a purchase. An additional advantage of custom labels is the ability to make separate bids for different products depending on which ones are the better sellers, which ones bring in higher profits for your business, which ones are currently available, on sale, and so on.

Shopping Feed

The way that a product is displayed is just as important to your potential profits as the quality of the product itself. Online shopping is highly competitive because of the much wider range of products available as compare to brick and mortar stores. You need to make sure that your shopping feed is the best that it can be to make your products stand out.

The attention span of the average customer today is shorter than ever before. Most people will give a single product a few short seconds before passing it over. You may still be able to sell some product without optimizing your feed, but you will lose out on a lot of sales. If you can capture the attention of today's ultra-impatient shopper, you may be able to improve your sales drastically. Learn how to show shoppers what they want to see and deliver it in a format that takes as little time as possible to absorb. Then you can win them over and maximize the resources that you have put into Google Shopping.

It today's market, good enough is never good enough. Businesses must utilize every platform available and provide high quality products to shoppers to grow. Your potential customers are not looking for something that is good enough. You must offer them something extraordinary. Anything less is a huge waste of time and ad capital.

Part 2:
Amazon Vendor Central

How to Become an Amazon Vendor

Fulfillment by Amazon (FBA) and fulfillment by merchant (FBM) are not the only Amazon business models. The Amazon Vendor program is where Amazon buys products wholesale directly from you and sells your product on the Amazon platform. You may have noticed these products on the Amazon platform before with the tagline "Ships from and sold by Amazon.com." There are many pros and cons to being an Amazon vendor. Here, we will focus on how to become an Amazon Vendor.

The Invitation-Only Party

Unfortunately, the Amazon Vendor program is offered on an invitation only basis. There are a few ways that you could have an invitation extended to you. Each product category on Amazon has buyer reps that are responsible for managing relationships and orders with their suppliers for their specific category. These buyer reps are also the ones responsible for inviting companies, brands and sellers to the Amazon Vendor program. They make the invitations based on whether they believe your product would sell well for Amazon.

If you are a well-recognized brand, chances are you will receive an invitation from Amazon for the vendor program. Amazon wants to have the largest brands on their platform and will work to have your products sold by Amazon. Alternatively, Amazon buyers may also invite you to the Vendor program if you are using the FBA or FBM model with products that are selling well in their category. Top sellers will generally receive an email from Amazon at some point asking if they are interested in joining Amazon Vendor Central and wholesaling to Amazon.

Amazon buyers are also regularly on the road at trade shows looking for new products that they believe could do well, or products that they believe will compete with top sellers that are FBA or FBM. We've attended multiple tradeshows in the past few months and have met many different Amazon buyers making the rounds. This is another great way to get access to the vendor program.

There is one last way that you can be become an Amazon Vendor. You could request an invitation from an Amazon buyer! There is hope for all FBA and FBM sellers that want to go this route! Your request to become an Amazon vendor will be reviewed by Amazon buyer reps and the invitation will be offered or you will never hear anything again about it. The best chance of receiving an invitation when you request one is if your product is a top seller on Amazon, your account health is good and you have an established track record of selling on Amazon.

The Amazon vendor program is not right for every seller and faces different obstacles from the FBA or FBM business model. It is important to take the factors into consideration when thinking of becoming an Amazon Vendor.

Becoming an Amazon Vendor with Vendor Express

Amazon has another platform available for sellers looking to become an Amazon Vendor. The Amazon Vendor Express program is an opt-in program that sellers can utilize to become an Amazon vendor without having to go through the formal invitation process of the Vendor program. This can be a great transition for Fulfillment by Amazon (FBA) and Fulfillment by Merchant (FBM) sellers to become an Amazon Vendor with Vendor Express.

What is Amazon Vendor Express?

Vendor Express advertises this program saying "You sell us your products and we take care of the rest – from promoting and shipping to customer service and returns." It's not quite as simple as that, but that gives a good overview of the program. While Vendor Express can lead to purchase orders from Amazon for your products, it primarily serves a drop shipping function for Amazon. As part of the initial application to the Vendor Express program you need to "donate" or provide free samples of inventory to Amazon to test the market demand for your product. **During this trial period, you receive no money from Amazon and the inventory is essentially an investment into becoming a vendor. If the product does not sell, or sells slowly and you do not get accepted in vendor express you are out the money for the product.**

Amazon Vendor Express makes your products eligible for free two-day shipping for prime members and free shipping over the order threshold for non-prime members. Amazon will handle the shipping if the product is already in stock at a distribution center or will pay you for the two-day shipping if the product is leaving from your warehouse.

The Benefits of Vendor Express

The vendor express program does have a few benefits to sellers. The primary benefit is skipping the invitation process to become a vendor. Opting-in to the vendor program gives you a better opportunity to get your product picked up by Amazon on a long-term basis. If your product sells well, you will continue to receive purchase orders form Amazon and possibly be asked by Amazon to be a vendor for other products you may sell. The free two-day shipping from Amazon is also a huge selling point for your product – particularly if you are currently using the FBM program. From working with our clients, we have been able to see the difference that two-day shipping makes in conversion rates and, more importantly, product sales.

Another great benefit is selling with the Amazon branding on your product. This product will be reflected as "Shipped from and Sold by Amazon.com" on your product listing. Many customers look for this on listings as a sign of product quality. Customers believe that Amazon will only sell high quality products and will be more likely to purchase your product. **Vendor Express sellers also receive access to Amazon Marketing Services (AMS)**. This interface can be used to run sponsored ads, product detail page ads and, our favorite, banner ads. These powerful marketing tools can give you the ability to increase your visibility dramatically.

Amazon Vendor Express can be a good solution to sellers looking to become vendors to Amazon. Acceptance into the program is not guaranteed, however it is much easier than getting into the full-time Amazon Vendor Program. Being a vendor for Amazon does come with distinct disadvantages.

The Pros and Cons of Amazon Vendor Express

Amazon Vendor Express presents some great opportunities for sellers to move into the vendor space with Amazon. The Amazon platform continues to be the fastest growing ecommerce platform and offers incredible opportunities to sell you products however, as with anything, there are some pros and cons to Amazon Vendor Express. We are going to be discussing the advantages and disadvantages of Amazon Vendor Express.

The Pros of Amazon Vendor Express

There are a few great features about Amazon Vendor Express that make it an interesting opportunity for many companies looking to transition from using Amazon Seller Central to Vendor Central. One of the best perks of this program is access to Amazon Marketing Services (AMS). AMS provides sellers unique opportunities to advertise their products. You can run ads like the pay-per-click (PPC) ads in Seller Central or choose to run product display ads or banner ads as a Vendor. This can give you a great leg up on competition utilizing Fulfillment by Amazon (FBA) or Fulfillment by Merchant (FBM). Increased product visibility is one of the great features of being a vendor with Vendor Express and vendors now can create A+ detail pages.

Another great perk is not having to worry about customer service – at all. Amazon customer service reps handle all inquiries regarding products, returns and refunds. This alone will give you more time to focus on running and growing your business. Remember, under this model you are shifting from the retail side to the wholesale side so you are only dealing with your distributors (Amazon) and not your end users (customers).

Fulfillment of your product can be handled in two ways. Amazon may want to place purchase orders for large quantities and have the inventory in house. The other option would involve Amazon drop shipping from you – so receiving an order and sending to you to be shipped out. Amazon pays the cost of product shipping and your product is automatically eligible free two-day shipping for prime members. This can help your product stand out from the FBM competition. Your product listings will also say "Shipped from and Sold by Amazon.com" which can give your listing much more credibility in the eyes of the consumer.

One last great pro of the Amazon Vendor Express program is it's free! Yes, Vendor Express is free compared to the monthly payments for a professional seller account with Amazon. It's a small savings on monthly basis, but everything helps!

The Cons of Vendor Express

Being a wholesale distributor to Amazon means that you will see your product margins decreased. You would be selling a higher volume to Amazon at a lower (wholesale) price. The trade-off here is being able to move more product at a lower price – however that may not mean you are making more profits. Unless you believe your product demand will increase drastically by having the additional AMS marketing benefits and Amazon branding, it may make more sense to continue selling your product yourself at retail prices.

Another negative of the Vendor Express program is that there is no guarantee that Amazon will pick up your product. Amazon may request that you send an order of inventory for free to test your product out. Amazon wants to make sure that they will make money from your product so this trial period is usually unavoidable. The manufacturer or seller needs to look at it as an investment into becoming an Amazon vendor. Unfortunately, if your product does not move or does not move as well as Amazon would like, they will decide not to pick your product up and you are out the money for the test order.

The final negative is that Amazon vendor payments are on a Net 60 basis. This means that sellers do not have readily accessible money coming back from Amazon on a regular basis. Amazon will also take a discount if it pays the invoices before the 60 days which can also decrease the revenue coming back to you.

It is important for sellers looking to transition to being a vendor to consider all the positive and negatives involved. It may not make sense for every business and Seller Central may be the best platform for you.

Launch on European Marketplace through Vendor Express

Amazon has expanded into Europe, opening up five markets that eCommerce businesses can tap. Amazon Vendor Central is open by invitation only, but anyone is free to join Vendor Express, which has some features that are like Vendor Central. Vendors with an Amazon North America account can enter the European market to sell on the Amazon marketplaces in Germany, France, Spain, Italy, and the UK. The steps to joining Vendor Express are simple, and being a member offers several advantages:

1. Access Amazon Marketing Services (AMS) and other tools for selling. AMS opens access to Sponsored Products and other ads, content optimization options, and sales reports. *

2. Sell your products to the hundreds of millions of online shoppers who search on Amazon.

3. Get a better chance to win the buy-box and ride on the Amazon name since your product listings will be marked as "Sold by Amazon".

4. Sell to Amazon and let them take care of merchandising, order handling, shipping, returns and 24/7 customer service. **

5. Get free shipping for your products to Amazon from your warehouse.

6. Store your products for free at Amazon's warehouses.

7. Offer your products to customers with free shipping for above minimum orders and free 2-day shipping for Prime customers.

   *   *Vendor Express does not grant regular access to A+ content, and does not offer the premium analytics that is available on Vendor Central.*

   **   *Fulfillment options include FBA, where Amazon takes care of inventory and shipping cost, and Direct Fulfillment (drop-ship), where Amazon sends you a prepaid and pre-filled form for shipping directly to customers. You must choose one or the other, and will not have the freedom to switch back and forth.*

Before registering to Vendor Express, you should be aware of a few things:

- You can submit a selling price offer (the MSRP), but the pricing of your products will be automated and controlled by Amazon.

- Purchase orders from Amazon will also be automated, which can result in issues with out-of-stock items when estimates are inaccurate.

- You will not be able to negotiate the terms of your contract with Amazon.

- You will not be able to use a manufacturer badge for comments on customer reviews.

Join the European Marketplace

To enter the European Marketplace as a vendor, you will need a Vendor Express account. As soon as you sign up, you can start selling your products to Amazon. Note that you cannot use a Vendor Central account for Vendor Express If you already have a personal Amazon account, you can sign in with this same email address and password. Amazon recommends, however, that you set up a separate account for Vendor Express:

1. On the Vendor Express homepage, click "Sign Up" in the upper right hand corner.

2. Type in the name of your business, your business email address, physical address and phone number. Add your VAT ID and complete bank account information – bank, branch, account name, IBAN and SWIFT/BIC, etc.

3. Add the products that you want to sell to Amazon.

4. Accept the Vendor Express <u>Terms and Conditions</u>.

5. Wait for a request from Amazon for free sample units and send them to Amazon. ***

6. Wait for your first purchase order from Amazon and send them the products.

*** When you enter into a vendor arrangement with Amazon, the company will require you to send them a number of free sample units. Amazon uses these product samples to test how well your product sells on the marketplace. Once they determine that there is a demand for your product, they will make their first purchase order form you and will likely order in bulk moving forward.

Products Eligible for Sale

Amazon is always adding new departments and categories to their marketplace. Currently, vendors can sell the products on this extensive <u>list</u>. Note that there is quite a list of products that are restricted to Vendor Express members on the Amazon UK marketplace.

Amazon Vendor Agreements

Receiving an invitation to become an Amazon vendor or thinking about signing up for Amazon Vendor Express is an exciting step for any product. With the recent global expansion of Amazon and plans to grow even further in 2017, the platform opens access to billions of potential customers. Amazon Vendor Agreements can be tricky, however. A full understanding of what your options are is key to setting up and maintaining a comfortable relationship with the online giant. If you are a potential vendor looking to tap the Amazon market or an experienced vendor seeking a more beneficial arrangement, read on for information and tips on how you can negotiate the vendor agreement that suits you best.

What a Vendor Agreement Means

When you enter a direct relationship with Amazon, you sell them your products as a wholesaler and they become a full-time distributor. A vendor agreement makes Amazon the legal owner of any product they order from you. Amazon then takes care of most of the marketing, merchandising, and pricing of those products. This takes much of the burden off you, and you agree to give Amazon your best wholesale price and fulfill your part in shipping what they order to their fulfillment centers.

In addition, Amazon vendor agreements may include cash consideration, which consist of cooperative marketing reimbursements, rebates, and the like. Amazon looks at these as reductions of what they pay for products. They generally apply when Amazon meets minimum purchase thresholds, which they estimate based on past performance and forecasts for the current year.

Vendor Agreement Benefits

By entering a vendor agreement with Amazon, you can benefit from their reach, reputation, advanced analytics, and premium services. Amazon boasts hundreds of millions of active customer accounts around the world. Even if you are not ready to launch your products globally, your vendor agreement opens global access to your products managed by Amazon. Amazon is fast becoming the go-to place for online shopping; not only in North America but also in Europe. Soon Asia could join the ranks of loyal Amazon shoppers. The Amazon experience continues to build customer trust which you can take advantage of with a vendor agreement. Your listings will show as Shipped and Sold by Amazon, leveraging that trust in their logistics and customer service reputation.

As Amazon has grown over the years, it has developed a powerful system for collecting and analyzing customer data. Your vendor agreement gives you access to that data, helping you to better understand customer behavior. This system combines with premium services such as Lightning Deals, A+ Content, and targeted email campaigns that increase visibility. These various marketing and merchandising services available to Amazon vendors can significantly boost sales. Amazon Prime is the icing on the cake. It gives customers the free shipping option on your product listings.

Know Your Options

Before considering becoming an Amazon vendor, there are a few things that you need to be prepared for. First, you need to have a warehouse in the US where Amazon can conveniently pick up product. Second, you need to barcode your products with their valid UPCs and/or an ASIN-embedded barcode. These are Amazon requirements. Third, you need to know within what bounds you can negotiate the terms of your vendor agreement. This includes such aspects as accruals, setting up new items, optimizing listings, streamlining operations, and troubleshooting. You may be considering setting up a new vendor agreement or terminating an existing one. Before you decide on either, it is vitally important that you know your options for negotiating trading terms and fees.

Accepting Amazon's proposed terms at face value can be a big mistake. Many times these vendor agreements prove unfavorable and may even be completely intolerable in the long run. In the excitement to join Amazon, many do not realize how much they are setting themselves up to lose. It is much more sensible to carefully review the terms beforehand to ensure that you are getting a deal that you will be happy with one, five, and even ten years down the line.

Balance is the Key

Amazon is in business just as much as any would-be vendor on the platform. Any counter-proposal that you offer must therefore remain beneficial to Amazon. If your suggestions on the vendor agreement do not bring value to the Amazon marketplace, your application will not be accepted.

The Proper Approach

The vendor agreement is a partnership and this entails getting to know the people you will be dealing with. Vendor Managers, also known as buyers, have their own primary goals laid out before them when they assess new vendor agreements.

The first thing to note is that they have their hands full and you will get a better response if you clearly and concisely communicate your proposed terms.

Second, Amazon Buyers are geared towards furthering Amazon's drive to be the go-to spot for any product. You will do well to show them that you can add to their selection with quality variations, unique products, and ASINs that are in high demand.

Third, Vendor Managers will always pay closer attention to the accounts that hold greater potential for Amazon. If you can show them your profitability, you have a greater chance of successfully negotiating your seller fees.

Before you contact Amazon to propose alternate terms, make sure that you have already decided your minimum offer, your middle ground, and your solid bottom line so that you know what wiggle room you have at every turn. Remember what leverage you have so that you can offer concessions that will grab and hold Amazon's attention. In addition to the qualities of your products, good press coverage, and participation in marketing campaigns, promotions and merchandising can tip the scales in your favor. Finally, note that the best time to open negotiations with Amazon is near the time when your vendor agreement is due for renewal.

Items to Negotiate

Not everything on your vendor agreement is flexible. You are most likely to get somewhere in your negotiations if you ask for changes on cost price, allowances, accruals, returns, freight, and payment terms.

First, look at the sum of your cost prices and allowances before you settle allowances and accruals. Some adjustments can be made in costs if Amazon asks for more allowances. Amazon will want to get several types of accruals and allowances, such as marketing, damages, freight and Subscribe and Save (SNS), depending on the agreed product category, freight, and return rights. Amazon will push here to meet their minimums.

Second, press for no returns or at least a lower rate on overstock before you sign off on full return rights on undamaged overstock. You will likely have to accept full returns on defective products and those damaged by the carrier, but not for warehouse damaged returns.

Third, Amazon can be flexible on prepaid or collect for freight. Fourth, Amazon will ask for the longest possible payment terms, but you can resist to get shorter payment terms that will be better for your business. Amazon will be more likely to agree if you can give them a quick pay discount, even if it is as little as 1% for payments made within sixty days from the date of invoice.

Fifth, try to follow the system that is laid out in the vendor agreement, for instance, how payment dates are counted. Understanding how they word things can save you a lot of headache.

Keep in Mind

Whatever points you are trying to negotiate or re-negotiate, remember that you will be in a much better position to get things to swing your way if you have a good relationship with your Vendor Manager. If you are in a very tough position and you are considering cancelling your vendor agreement, make sure that you are willing to leave Amazon if you are set on taking an aggressive stance with them. Be clear about what you are risking in any case, and do not use last-resort tactics such as stopping all orders to push Amazon to enter negotiations unless you are serious. At the end of the day, however, maintaining good relations with Amazon will benefit you even if you will no longer be selling on the platform.

Vendor Central Set-Up

Amazon's Vendor Setup Process is a bit long and can be somewhat confusing, particularly in the areas of New Items Setup (NIS) and Commitment Plans. Below we are going to take you through the initial account setup to make sure that no steps were missed, then go through the particulars of getting your NIS optimized, and adding your products to a Commitment Plan.

Setting Up Your Vendor Account

The first thing to do is to make sure that you have properly completed the first steps to set up your vendor account to begin doing business with Amazon. Review the steps below to see if there is anything you may have missed or need to update.

1. If you have not received confirmation regarding your account within the prescribed timeframe, contact Amazon to follow up.

2. If you have not yet completed the setup process, sign in to Vendor Central as a new vendor and begin setting up your account.

3. If you already have access with the email and password that you entered during the setup process, you should be able to log in to Vendor Central.

4. Locate the Show Your Progress table on the Setup Process Welcome. Check in what stage you are for each module and the steps that you need to take to move forward:

    -   Incomplete – Enter the required information. Some of this concerns Accepting terms and agreements, adding banking information, adding contacts, adding return addresses, and adding warehouse addresses.

    -   Pending Amazon Action – Waiting on Amazon, no action required. Check back later to verify that the module is Completed, and enter any required information if it is Incomplete.

    -   Completed – Access this module to review your information and make any necessary updates.

5. When all your modules are complete, make sure that you have submitted them for final approval. Locate the Submit for Final Approval button to do this. Once approved, your ordering re-

lationship with Amazon is established and you can proceed to do business.

6. Update your contact information, credentials, warehouse addresses, new users and user permissions under the Settings

Optimize Your New Items Setup

As a new Amazon Vendor, you can manage most areas of your account and orders from your account home page. One of the first steps at this point is to add your products to the Amazon catalog by creating ASINs. Before you do so, however, there are a few steps to ensure that your items are optimized. Taking the time to do your NIS correctly is vitally important to avoid customer dissatisfaction, barcode and delivery errors, item unavailability, and grave pricing mishaps.

Note here that all your product information should be saved in a spreadsheet, whether it is an offline document or in Google Drive, or in a database that you have prepared for this purpose.

Optimize Your Items

1. Check your UPCs/EANs/GTINs to make sure that each of your products has a unique barcode at the consumer packaging level and not just the master carton identifier. Check also that the proper consumer barcode is labeled on the packaging per Amazon standards.

2. Download and review the Amazon Setup Form to familiarize yourself with how different product titles are created. Some forms will combine information from different columns while others will permit you to enter your desired product title or suggest an alternate product title. In some cases, strict compliance with the <Brand><Model Number><Product Title>, <Size>, <Color> format is observed. Maximize the available

flexibility in your product title for readability and to get your relevant keywords indexed in Amazon's search engine.

3. Take some time to compose compelling bullet points for each product. These key features and benefits of your product are what will entice a shopper to read more about your product. Use the third person voice and speak plainly about your product without exaggerations. Explain why the product is good and what value it has.

4. Add a description in the same manner, putting in more keywords that will help shoppers find your listing. Compose your sentences in a positive and matter-of-fact tone, avoiding the sales pitch.

5. Have professional images done and optimize them for mobile. Most shoppers are using the Amazon app so they need to be able to see your product clearly on their mobile devices. Keep your images in online storage to prevent artifacts and name them by UPC code.

Process Your Items

Now you are ready to begin the New Items Setup (NIS).

1. Check your template to make sure that it is ready for upload.

2. Navigate to the Items tab to begin adding your products and uploading your images. Each product should have at least one image.

3. If you get errors from Vendor Central, check the mandatory fields again and re-upload.

4. Request variations of styles such as color or size on a single page. This will aggregate reviews and improve the search relevance of your listing and the shopping experience of your

customers. Check the attributes that you select so that bullet points and images will change as shoppers click or use drop-downs to see the different choices. Download and browse the Variation template from the Resource Center to become familiar with how it works.

5. Review what you have so far to make sure that it comes out the way you intended. Sometimes, what shows up on Amazon does not follow as you entered it on the NIS form. Make sure your product information, variation sets, and images are correct and render nicely.

6. Build your Amazon ASINs in Vendor Central to retain control over the content. If you allow third party sellers to build ASINs, you will not have much control over its content, including bullet points and descriptions. To ensure that you maintain control, don't release your setup information to any channels until you have assigned ASINs from Amazon. When third party sellers do this setup, they will likely use your UPC and part number, and Amazon will assign that ASIN to your Vendor code. Third party sellers may use a different UPC and this will create a separate page and ASIN. This means more trouble for you as you must create a ticket to get this manually merged into your page and your ASIN.

7. Amazon will process your submission, troubleshoot errors, and create your ASINs. When the process is complete, you will receive a notification.

When you are done uploading your new items, give Amazon three to five days before you check if they are live. Within another few days, Amazon should place an order. Note that Amazon prefers Electronic Data Interchange (EDI) integration for exchanging order-related information. If your company is or might soon be integrated, visit the Technical tab of the Resource Center to get familiar with EDI. One benefit of EDI is that you will no longer need to provide warehouse address information to send the EDI 856 document. Note also that with EDI, your freight terms are set to Prepaid.

Add Products to a Commitment Plan

You can add products to the Amazon catalog for an existing commitment plan. You may also be eligible to add product details for an existing commitment plan. Below are the steps.

1. Navigate to Items and Add Products in Vendor Central, and select what action you want to process; add commitment plan products or add details for commitment plan products.

2. Select a Template to work with and navigate to the Commitment Plans. Choose the commitment plan that you want. Alternatively, click the box in the header row to select all commitment plans listed in the table. Select the version of Microsoft Office that you are using and download the template, or click Import products from Inovis.

3. Save your downloaded Excel template. Do not change the default file extension. Open the template and add any missing product details. When you are done making additions, click the Amazon menu and Validate Template. Review once more for errors and save the template.

4. Go back to vendor Central and navigate to the Add Products Click Browse, select the template file, and Submit file.

Once you have submitted your file, all you need to do is wait for Amazon to confirm and you are all set.

Working with your Amazon Vendor Manager

One very important key to the growth of your Amazon business is in the hands of your vendor manager. This is especially true if you do not have Strategic Vendor Services. To progress, you need to develop a good working relationship with your vendor manager. We are going to share some tips with you on just how to do that. First, it is crucial to understand what vendor managers do on a daily basis and how much of it they have on their plates. Then you can approach them with a better perspective and apply a few strategies to get the ball rolling.

What Vendor Managers Do

The first step to understanding how best to deal with your vendor manager is knowing where they are coming from. Vendor managers are extremely busy people who worked hard to get where they are and even harder to stay there. Vendor managers work very long hours, juggle multiple tasks on tens of thousands of accounts, and struggle with extremely tight deadlines. Hands down, vendor managers have the toughest job of the three retail teams.

Vendor managers are responsible for managing all aspects of the categories that they are assigned to. They answer for sales, profits and losses, marketing, promotions, negotiations with vendors, and customer experience. Vendor managers work with one foot in day-to-day operations and the other in long-term strategic planning. They are often dealing with several departments at once, including buying, marketing, site merchandising, finance, retail systems and public relations. Amazon is nothing if not results-oriented and vendor managers are expected to perform at a high level at every turn.

The primary focus of vendor managers is developing strategies for negotiating with vendors and building long-term relationships with strategic partners. Vendor managers must show constant improvements to hit sales and margin targets. As a vendor, you must get on this page to warrant the attention of your vendor manager.

Lastly, Amazon runs an MBA rotation program that takes fresh graduates and puts them in a rotation. If you have been a vendor for some time, you may have experienced having a vendor manager and then having a new one come in and try to pick up where the previous one left off. These new MBAs are being pulled from one team to the next every 18 months – vendor managers, buying and inventory, and marketing and merchandising. Some will work out better than others and you will simply have to roll with it. Try to be understanding when a new vendor manager is assigned to you. They might not get it entirely right in the beginning, but your patience will pay off as you build a good relationship with them from the outset.

Building the Relationship

As a vendor, you are likely focused on several aspects of growing your Amazon business. You might be looking for category guidance, wanting to negotiate better terms for your vendor agreement, or trying to get in on bulk buys or large merchandising campaigns. Whether it is a simple matter or a huge move, you need to have a solid partnership with your vendor manager. Strengthening this link is vital to your success and here's how you can achieve just that.

Handle Small Tasks Yourself

If you are having a bunch of smaller issues, don't go straight to your vendor manager with them. Try as much as possible to handle these issues through Vendor Central support. Remember, your vendor manager is very busy and will not take kindly to being bombarded with these small matters. Getting things done though Vendor Central can be frustrating, but you want to keep as much of that as you can away from your vendor manager. They will be more willing to help when you do contact them and be ready to help you with the bigger issues. This way, when you do need them to step in if you are getting nowhere with support they will know that you are honestly having trouble and will be more willing to get things going.

Baby Steps

You might be tempted to explain everything that you have in mind in one long, albeit carefully crafted email. This is not a good way to communicate with your vendor manager. Vendor managers typically must get through hundreds of emails every day, so prioritizing is essential to their survival. Long emails are hard to digest. Sorting through them to be able to prioritize the items in there that need immediate attention is exceedingly tedious. Keep your messages short and sweet to help your vendor manager to get it processed and forwarded faster to the appropriate team. If you need several things acted upon send them separately. Even ten separate messages with clear subject lines are better than one if the items in them are divided logically. And don't forget that vendor managers are people too. They have their own quirks when it comes to how they work so it doesn't hurt to ask them what works best. And always remember to thank them even before they have processed your request.

Spend on Marketing

You may not have been prepared to release funds just yet. Your vendor manager is, however, looking at the numbers. To put it simply, your vendor manager is interested in how profitable your ASINs are. A good way to start a conversation with your vendor manager is to go straight to the numbers. Ask their advice on where to invest. This is a concise move in line with their goals that proves that you are serious about growing your business in partnership with them as category experts. Be ready to bring out a few thousand dollars for a campaign and watch your vendor manager's interest grow. Then you can work with them on unique marketing opportunities Amazon may have available.

Add Variety

Vendor managers are always looking for vendors who can add value to Amazon. They want to see growth in the category that they manage which means products that expand the available selection. If you haven't updated your selection recently, now is the best time to do so. Look at what you have and what you can add to it that will improve your category. Check your items and make sure that they are all properly listed and not marked as Off Season or Obsolete, for example. Look also at what other brands and fresh items you can make available to Amazon retail. Then set up a meeting with your vendor manager to talk about developing virtual bundles.

Meet and Greet

We live in a virtual world, but there really is no substitute for human contact. If you can squeeze it into your schedule, join a Seattle category summit every now and again. These meet-ups tend to get the creative juices flowing and you might also get some good ideas from them on how to refocus your efforts. Not only will you learn a lot, but you will also get a chance to talk to your Amazon team at a personal level. Getting to know a little more about them and even just being able to give them a real smile and a handshake can go a long way. They will appreciate the effort and remember you, and this will always be good when those new programs and campaign opportunities come around.

These are just a few ways that you can cultivate a better working relationship with your vendor manager. Every vendor manager is different and you may have to adjust here and there, but keeping these basic principles in mind can help you maintain a good balance and get through tough spots.

How to Use Amazon Vendor Central Promotions & Coupons to Generate Sales

One of the challenges of growing on the Amazon Vendor Central platform is generating demand for your product. Vendors have a variety of options that they can use within Amazon Vendor Central – from marketing to promotional services. They are also able to request access to Amazon Seller Central to drive sales. We are going to discuss the many Amazon Vendor Central Promotions that you as a vendor have access to. Combining these promotions with advertising can create a strong Amazon Vendor Central marketing strategy that will increase your purchase orders from Amazon.

What types of promotions can I create on Vendor Central?

There are currently three types of promotions that vendors can offer through Amazon Vendor Central. Each promotion can be used to impact your products sales. The promotions boost your products' visibility on Amazon, and can improve your product ranking through lower pricing. Effective pricing provides the benefit of increased conversions, page views and ordered items. Promotions also allow your product to be sold for less without having to adjust your cost to Amazon. Amazon looks for ways to push their costs down. It is more than likely if you every drop your cost to Amazon you will not be able to increase it again in the future. Promotions allow you to temporarily drop your product's retail price without having to adjust your cost.

Lightning deals are available in both the Vendor Central and Seller Central platforms. These promotions have the most visibility on the "Today's Deals" page and run for up to 6 hours. Amazon requires that the promotion be at least 20% off to be accepted. You can limit the amount of inventory you want sold. After all the promotional units have been added to a cart, your offer appears with a button that says "Join Waitlist" in case a customer who has currently claimed the promotion removes it from their cart. Lightning deals can provide quick sales boosts for your product, but this may not be enough to provide a long-term benefit. These are our least preferred deals to run for our clients. **The lack of clarity around any long-term benefits and needing to provide a substantial discount to maximize visibility makes it difficult to justify the value of these promotions.**

Best deal promotions provide much more value for the discount provided. The product still appears on the "Today's Deals" pages and can be run for up to 2 weeks. You can add multiple products within a single Best deal promotion. This allows you to feature your entire catalog or complimentary products at discounts. One listing will show up as the discount and when a customer clicks on the offering it will bring them to a page that features all your offered discounts within the Best deal promotion. **We prefer these types of promotions for our clients.** The product gets additional visibility by being on the "Today's deals" page and you can employ an Amazon Marketing Services (AMS) campaign to maximize visibility on search engine results pages (SERPs). The increased conversions, page views and orders can greatly increase your products' relevancy within the Amazon A9 algorithm, and provide great long-term sales benefits.

Price discount promotions also provide great value. This type of promotion does not appear on the "Today's Deals" page – the promotion only appears on the product listing itself. These promotions can be approved within as short as 24 hours and can run for a maximum of 5 weeks. We've previously discussed the effects that pricing can have within the A9 algorithm. Effective pricing of your product (in the form of a discount) can boost your products visibility on Amazon. **By partnering these promotions with a AMS campaign you can greatly impact the relevancy of your product.** The increased page views and conversions can boost your product up the SERPs and can lead to great long-term sales benefits. These Amazon Vendor Central Promotions are great ways to improve your purchase orders from Amazon.

How can I use coupons to boost my products sales?

Coupons are the other type of Amazon Vendor Central Promotions available. Coupon promotions charge small fees every time the coupon is clipped and redeemed, in addition to the discount that is provided. Coupon promotions are featured on the "Coupons" page within the "Today's Deal" page. These also appear on the product display page and on the SERPs. Multiple products can be submitted for coupons at the same time. You can also limit the number of coupons redeemed per customer or only make the coupons available when a customer signs up for "Subscribe and Save."

One unique feature of coupons is the Coupon Landing Page (CLP). CLPs are created when a coupon promotion is submitted within Vendor Central. These landing pages are great for off-site marketing campaigns. You can utilize a CLP within an email marketing campaign or social media marketing campaign. The CLPs are within social media sites like Facebook's advertising Terms of Service and can be used to drive more traffic to your page. We typically employ ad campaigns leading directly to the CLP from sites such as Facebook. The additional traffic and sales can improve your products' ranking within Amazon and provide long-term sales benefits as well.

Now that you have a better understanding of the Amazon Vendor Central Promotions you can employ these same strategies to boost your products sales. These strategies can lead to long-term purchase orders from Amazon and sustained success on the Amazon platform. Finding the right strategy for your product is important. Be sure to consider all the costs to you and compare it to the future benefits to see if these are right for you.

Amazon A+ Detail Pages

Vendors can utilize Amazon A+ Detail pages through the Vendor Central interface. The A+ Detail Pages allow vendors to include extra content in their product listings to help promote their products. This feature was only available to vendors using the Vendor Central interface, but is now available to Vendor Express users as well. The added rich content can make your product standout from your competitions listings, however this option does come at an extra cost to vendors. We recommend the A+ Detail Pages option to many of our vendor clients and help them implement effective rich content into their listings.

What are the benefits of A+ Detail Pages?

In our experience, A+ Detail Pages have helped increase our clients' sales by 5%-20%. That should be reason enough to consider using these pages in your listings. There are other reasons to consider using A+ Detail Pages as well.

Vendors can create enhanced product description pages giving them a leg-up on their competition. These pages can be customized with paragraphs, images, charts and other features that make listings pop and provide unique opportunities to connect with customers. This allows the listing to convey a greater sense of value to the customer which can greatly increase customer conversion rates. These pages also allow you to add much more text into your listing. These two factors can improve your organic search optimization since conversions rate play an important role in the Amazon algorithm and you can index for more keywords.

We recommend the use of A+ Detail Pages to our Vendor Central clients that are trying to educate the consumer about their product. You may have a product that is a great substitute for a competitor's product because of its features or ingredients, but the competitor may have more brand recognition in that specific category. An example could be a skin care product that contains additional vitamins or minerals that are beneficial, but absent from the competitor's product. A+ Detail Pages can also help you build brand awareness.

How do I create A+ Detail Pages?

Amazon currently has two options to create A+ Detail pages; build your own or have them build the page for you. The pricing to have Amazon build the pages varies on what type of premium services you are enrolled in vendor central with. Vendors that sign-up with the basic vendor central package pay $1500 per page. The finished page would apply to parent-child variations and a separate page is not required for each variation. Amazon also will not build pages for certain categories and marketplaces.

Building your own A+ Detail Page is another viable option for many vendors that have in-house design teams. The cost is much less at $600 per page and applies to all child variations. For vendors that do not have their own in-house design team, creating A+ Detail Pages can be rather time consuming. The A+ Detail Pages are built from modules that will require content to be created, uploaded and arranged to create the page design. We help many of our clients build great converting A+ Detail Pages that will bring them significant sales increases.

Resources

Freeeup
An outsourcing business that has affordable, highly skilled workers to help you focus on growing your business
www.freeeup.com

Upwork
A website for freelancers with all types of skills that can help you affordably outsource work
www.upwork.com

THE AMAZON VINE PROGRAM

Amazon Vine is another great program developed by Amazon to benefit their vendors. The program is open to vendor and vendor express users only, and allows vendors to access Amazon's top reviewers. Vine allows vendors to set-up deep product discounts for top reviewers in exchange for their fair and honest reviews. This allows vendors to launch their products with a significant number of product reviews – giving their product a level of social-proof that can help them convert Amazon shoppers into customers.

How does Amazon Vine work?

The Vine program works in two parts; the reviewer side and the vendor side. Membership for reviewers is on an invitation-only basis. Vine members, or Vine Voices as Amazon calls them, are invited based on the helpfulness of their reviews as judge by other Amazon members (the "Was this review helpful to you?" buttons at the bottom of a review) and their interest in the products being offered for review in the vine program. Amazon wants the Vine Voices to have a great reputation and expert knowledge of products in their specific product category. "Vine Voice" shows up as badge next to their name and is how you can distinguish your Vine reviews from organic customer reviews. Voices are required to submit reviews for the products within 30 days of receiving or risk having their account suspended.

Vendors can use the program by enrolling a product or ASIN into the program. Amazon will give you a price to list the product within the Vine program. **The price can range anywhere from $2500-$7500 based on the product category.** Amazon limits the amount of inventory that you can enroll in the program based on the category. In our experience, the limit is around 30 units per product. Once an ASIN is enrolled, Amazon will have you send the product to a distribution center to be distributed to Vine Voices. You can select when you want the product to be available to Vine Voices and Amazon will not place the product in queue until that date.

The Amazon Vine program is useful for vendors to garner reviews for their products. As we've mentioned before, reviews are the social-proof that can help you get more conversions. One of the unique features of the Vine program is a vendor's ability to enroll pre-launch products. This can allow a vendor to gain a slight advantage on competition by starting with product reviews from day one. We also believe that having reviews from top ranked reviewers on your listing is weighted heavier in the Amazon algorithm. At the very least, Vine Voices tend to write long reviews which can help you show up in search results with all the added keywords. The cost of the vendor program is certainly a drawback and may not make it worthwhile for each Amazon Vendor.

Amazon Marketing Services (AMS) Overview

Amazon Marketing Services is the advertising platform available to Amazon Vendors using both the Vendor Central and Vendor Express platforms. AMS provides great marketing opportunities for brands with three different ad types: **sponsored product ads; product display page ads; and, headline search ads.** These ads are based off keyword searches, related products and product trends. AMS is free for vendors to use and advertising spend is based on the number of clicks their ads get.

How does Amazon Marketing Services work?

AMS advertising campaigns are cost-per-click or pay-per-click (PPC) and are based off a budget you establish for the product. The minimum budget allowed is $100 and at least $1 a day, while the campaign is required to run for a minimum of 1 day. The campaigns can be created with 3 different ad types that determine how your ads will be seen.

The first ad type is sponsored products which is like the sponsored product campaigns available in Seller Central. The ads will appear in the search results list and are based off keywords that are included in each campaign. Like seller central, these ads can be set to automatic or manual targeting. Match types can be set to broad, phrase, exact, negative phrase and negative exact. All keywords are included throughout the entire campaign and cannot be grouped into Ad Groups.

The next ad type is product display page ads. These are powerful ads that you can utilize to compete directly with competitors and top sellers in the category. They can also be useful if your product is complementary to a target product. The ads will appear on the side or bottom of search results pages and on related product pages. Product display campaigns allow you to target competitors ASINs or broader shopper interests.

The final ad type, and our personal favorite, is the headline search ads. These are large banner ads that appear at the top of search results and ensure maximum visibility for your product. Headline search ads can utilize another powerful AMS feature in the form of landing pages – which we will discuss further. These ads allow you to feature multiple products across the banner ad. You can use the ad to redirect to these specific products or to a broader landing page for your entire brand. This is a great tool to gain brand visibility on Amazon.

Each of these ad types come with Performance Metrics like what exists in Amazon Seller Central. The metrics tracked are impressions, clicks, average cost per click, ad spend, estimated total sales and ACOS (average cost of sales). Campaigns can be quickly duplicated for A/B testing different aspects. AMS also features report downloads which can help you manipulate and analyze the data better in an Excel file. AMS does not have a bulk operations feature like Amazon Seller Central does which can make updating keyword bids slightly more tedious.

What is the Amazon Marketing Services Pages feature?

Amazon Pages are personalized landing pages for your brand and products on Amazon.com. The Amazon Pages feature is free to use in AMS, allows you to create an Amazon URL for your page *(i.e., amazon.com/YOURBRAND)*, highlight key products, and tell your brand's story. Amazon currently allows you to create one page per brand, but you can edit the page if you are attempting to push certain products as part of a campaign. They also have a powerful page metrics tool that can be used to track page views, customer engagement and potentially allow for re-targeting in the future.

Amazon Marketing Services is a powerful tool that many brands should be utilizing to grow their brand on Amazon. Achieving optimal performance with these marketing services is key to increasing the visibility and sales of your brand.

Marketing Via Amazon Media Group

Another great feature of AMS is the Amazon Media Group. AMG is a premium service that gives Amazon vendors additional chances to display their products in strategic positions on the platform. Amazon Media Group marketing opens opportunities for measurable cross-device campaigns with the Amazon Advertising Platform (AAP), Kindle, Fire tablet and Fire TV in addition to Amazon Display Ads. Shopping and media are innately interwoven in the online world and the research opportunity that AMG presents can prove invaluable to long-term marketing goals.

Let's look at a few ways in which Amazon Media Group services can help grow your business as a brand supplier to Amazon's retail business:

Amazon Advertising Platform

Amazon vendors can leverage this platform to reach more customers on additional Amazon sites and on third-party sites as well. The platform manages the optimum placement of video ads within the natural flow of content on a website and the insertion of full-screen pop-ups. Through these ad placements, AAP ads aim to generate better quality leads and redirect this targeted traffic to vendor web pages to encourage sales. The Amazon Advertising Platform is an ideal way for vendors to reach a wider audience through several placement options.

Kindle and Fire Experiences

Vendors can launch visual campaigns that target Amazon customers on Kindle, Fire tablet and Fire TV. These ads can be set to show in the Kindle and Fire tablets' lock screen mode and at the top of Fire TV home screens. Amazon reports that these ads are comparable to standard web-based campaigns in promoting brand awareness, and cost the same or less. Analytics are available for these ads to measure the ad's impact on shoppers throughout their browsing sessions.

In-stream Video Ads

This option allows in-stream video ads on the Amazon Ad Platform that meet the following criteria:

Aspect ratio (dimensions)	16:9 (640x360 px)
Frame rate	At least 15 FPs
Audio	128kbps / 44khz
Recommended bit rate	2Mbps
Preferred codec	Video: H.264, MPEG-2, or MPEG-4; Audio: MP3 or AAC
Recommended file size	100MB (larger sizes are supported but may require longer SLAs)
Video duration	5 to 30 seconds

Amazon recommends using VAST 2 third party video tags from an Amazon certified third party vendor to ensure wide support. VPAID tags can also be used if it employs both Flash and JavaScript, from the same approved vendors. Ad servers should use a properly formatted Cross Origin Resource Sharing (CORS) header to serve on Amazon-owned sites for security reasons.

Mobile App Banner Ads

Mobile Image Banner and Rich Media ads (limited to third-party sites) allow vendors to target a wider mobile audience by expanding their reach to third-party Android, iOS, and Kindle Fire apps. The specifications and requirements for these ads are:

Image Banner Ads

Ad Size	Creative Dimensions	Maximum File Weight	File Format
320 x 50	640 x 100 px @2X (required)	50 kb	JPG / PNG-8
300 x 250	600 x 500 px @2X	200 kb	JPG / PNG-8
728 x 90	1456 x 180 px @2x	200 kb	JPG / PNG-8
414x125	1242 x 375 px @3x (required)	100 kb	JPG / PNG-8

Rich Media Ads

Ad Size	Creative Dimensions @2X	Maximum Initial File Load	File Format
320 x 50	640 x 100 px (required)	100 kb	HTML
300 x 250	600 x 500 px	200 kb	HTML
728 x 90	1456 x 180 px	200 kb	HTML

Creative Guidelines

Image banner ads come in 320x50 pixels (2x resolution, 640x100px,) and 414x125 pixels (3x resolution, 1242x375,) for high resolution image quality. Other banner sizes should be at least 2x resolution for best results, but lower quality designs will be accepted by Amazon. 414x125 banner ads are for the Amazon app and mobile web platform specifically

The AdChoices label must be visible in one corner of each banner ad, to be automatically overlaid by Amazon. Banners can be linked to amazon but must have either the Amazon logo or text referencing Amazon on them. Vendors can refer to Amazon's AAP mobile app banner ads page for more details.

Mobile Interstitial Ads

Interstitial ads, or full screen ads covering an app interface, can be displayed along with banner ads on third-party apps. These ads can be positioned at key natural points in the content flow of a page to maximize wait times while avoiding interruptions that can distract and annoy shoppers. These ads are integrated with the use of the Mobile Ads API and can be easily closed by shoppers at any time.

Both the Medium Rectangle and the Full Screen Image interstitial ad templates are responsive to all mobile screen sizes and work on Android, iOS, and Fire. The Full Screen Image ad features one clickable image that is automatically resized for optimal display and minimal latency. This ad template allows for the addition of a video player in the center of the sized image where shoppers can play the video, access the action links above or below the video, or close the ad. Customer reviews can also be included in this ad, formatted with Amazon branded gold stars and 48-point Arial font, and showing the date that the rating was collected.

Amazon will automatically overlay a set AdChoices icon in the upper left corner and a prominent close button in the upper right corner of each ad. Vendors can visit Amazon's Mobile Interstitial Ads page for more information.

Desktop and Mobile Web Display Ads

The following standard ad sizes for display on Amazon and third party websites are available:

Ad Placement	Ad Size	Creative Dimensions (2x resolution or higher)	Max. File Weight	File Format
Medium Rectangle	300 x 250 px	300 x 250 px	200 kb HTML, 40 kb static (50 kb FR, IT, ES, JP)	JPG / PNG-8
Leaderboard	728 x 90 px	728 x 90 px	200 kb HTML, 40 kb static (50 kb FR, IT, ES, JP)	JPG / PNG-8
Wide Skyscraper	160 x 600 px	160 x 600 px	200 kb HTML, 40 kb static (50 kb FR, IT, ES, JP)	JPG / PNG-8
Large Rectangle	300 x 600 px	300 x 600 px	200 kb HTML, 50 kb static	JPG / PNG-8
Billboard	970 x 250 px, 800x250 pixels (DE)	970 x 250 px, 800x250 pixels (DE)	200 kb	JPG / PNG-8
Mobile Leaderboard	320 x 50 px	640 x 100 px @2X (required)	50 kb	JPG / PNG-8
Mobile Detail and Search Results page	414 x 125 px	1242 x 375 px @3X (required)	100 kb	JPG / PNG-8

Vendors can look at Amazon's mobile shopping details page for more on the Mobile Detail and Search Results page.

Amazon Media Group Tips

It is important to note that AMG is not specifically designed to boost vendors' ROI but to provide a means of analyzing market positioning and evaluating ad campaigns. AMG therefore requires a longer-term investment in brand awareness to build up to attaining the larger goal of capturing a bigger slice of market share. The minimum average investment required to make the most of AMG services is approximately $40,000 – a sum that requires serious thought and planning alongside alternative Amazon and third-party marketing options.

What is Amazon Retail Analytics Basic?

Amazon Retail Analytics Basic (ARA) is the primary reporting tool available to Amazon Vendors. Vendors will have access to these reports upon creating an Amazon Vendor Central account. As a vendor, you can use ARA to track your sales and inventory data, operational issues, stock levels, catalog quality and more. The access to the various reports depends on your permissions and the contract terms of your vendor agreement. In our opinion the ARA Basic reports are not as robust as the data you have access to as an Amazon third-party seller. There still is valuable data that can be extracted from the ARA Basic reports. We are going to cover the various reports here.

Sales and Inventory Reports

ARA Basic provides access to 3 different kinds of sales and inventory reports. The first report is the **Sales & Inventory Dashboard** which provides an overview of your Shipped Cost of Goods Sold (COGS) and on hand inventory at Amazon. It separates the information into four different time periods and provides period over period growth figures. The four time periods on the Sales & Inventory Dashboard are: Year-to-date, quarter-to-date, month-to-date and week-to-date.

The **Sales and Inventory Monthly Summary** report provides month-to-month data going back 25 periods. It allows you to view your Shipped COGS, on hand inventory values and quantities, and your open purchase order quantities.

The last and most valuable report is the **Sales and Inventory Product Details** report. This allows you to view sales and inventory data on a product by product basis. There are adjustable time frames to make it easier to view your products performance. This report allows you to see your best performing products and can provide valuable insight on how to grow your overall sales. For example, a variation or bundle with a strong performing product could be improved by optimization or advertising to see similar sales.

Demand Forecast

The **Demand Forecast** report is used for inventory planning purposes. The report estimates the purchase orders you will receive from Amazon based on a few factors. The main factor is the prior weeks' sales data; however, it also considers seasonal increases and Q4 data sales data from the prior year. This report only provides an educated guess from Amazon on what they may need. The quantities are by no means set in stone and subject to change.

Catalog Report

The Vendor Catalog Listing report shows every product you have sold to Amazon that has page views. It sorts your listings by the page view rank. This report provides useful insight into inventory metrics and allows you to update listings that are missing images. It also calls out other listing issues that your catalog may have. Finally, it includes a replenishment code which indicates if you can be expecting more purchase orders from Amazon for the product.

Operations Reports

The Operations reports are composed of 6 separate reports that provide great insight into your purchase orders, operational metrics and performance. Operational Metrics allows you to filter your performance on purchasing, receiving, lead time, inbound defects and fast track instock performance. There are separate reports that break down each one of these areas further.

Purchasing has the **Purchase Order (PO) Details** report and the **PO Item Details report**. The first report provides an overview of your purchasing data, such as units received and received fill rate. It details all purchase orders created during the prior 3 months and can help you spot trends, issues, and ways you can improve purchasing. The PO Item Details report breaks down this data on an item-by-item basis versus an entire catalog overview. Both reports also include your receiving rates, units received and other data.

The **Lead Time Details** report tracks the lead time to fulfill a purchase order from Amazon. Lead time is measured from the time Amazon submits a purchase order until the time the product arrives at an Amazon fulfillment center. The report breaks down every aspect of lead time from days to confirm a purchase order to number of shipping days.

The **Inbound Receipt Defects** report shows defects in products that arrive at the Amazon fulfillment center. It breaks the defects down into a few different categories including: units not on POs, units over requested quantity, units sent to incorrect fulfillment center, unconfirmed quantity, and damaged units. This can help you find shipping issues with your own business or carrier.

Amazon Retail Analytics Premium

Amazon Retail Analytics, or ARA, is Amazon's own analytics tool for comprehensive sales data. As a vendor, you want to have a good grasp of not only your sales volume but what exactly is driving those sales. ARA was built to provide you with performance insights on where your sales are coming from, the competition, your customers' behavior, and what shoppers seem to be interested in your products. Knowing all this business intelligence can be a big help in guiding you on what is working, what needs to be improved, and where to start making the necessary changes.

What is Amazon Retail Analytics?

Amazon Retail Analytics is one of Amazon's own analytical tools, with a free and a Premium version available to vendors. It functions as an add-on on Vendor Central that provides vendors with supplementary reporting. The ARA reports give vendors data in separate sections, which include Customer Behavior, Inventory, Marketing, Operations, Sales, and Trends. Amazon Retail Analytics provides more over twenty different reports which are customized for you based on your product categories. Some of these reports are:

Amazon Search Terms

1. Find new keywords that you can use in paid ads.

2. Test the keywords that you have in your paid search portfolio against the terms that customers actually use through recorded impressions and conversions.

3. Test your keywords' effectiveness for each product against the competition's products.

4. Analyze search trends by season and location.

Or, alternatively, you can view the report on Amazon Top 100 Search Terms to look at the worldwide results for the most searched keywords in your category.

Customer Reviews

1. Compare customer reviews per item over time with average ratings.

2. Compare lifetime data to report-specific periods.

Page Views and Conversion

1. See how much awareness you are generating with your pages.

2. Look at how well you are converting for each product.

3. Compare your detail page content versus other vendors.

4. Look at together with Category Conversions to track product performance by availability date.

Sales

There are several different reports relating to sales, and the reports can be sent straight to your sales data or data warehouse. Tracking specific sales becomes easy with these reports

You can find the following specific information in these reports:

Category Sales and Share, Top Items, and Sales History by Week

- Track category performance in general or per title and over time

- See your share of each category and its subcategories and track growth

- Compare your products' rank and unit growth against Amazon's fastest selling products

- Spot growing categories that you can leverage

- See your top 100 products per category by sales and units

- Track the products that drive performance

- Analyze marketing campaigns from performance data over time

Find and Use Amazon Retail Analytics

To locate ARA Premium, log in to your Vendor central account and navigate to Reports. Locate Amazon Retail Analytics Premium on the list and click on it. If you are unable to see ARA, this means that you do not yet have access to these premium reports and must use the Basic version or sign up for the Premium one.

If you opt to subscribe to Amazon Retail Analytics Premium, you must sign up for the Vendor Premium Services package. The annual payment for this package runs from a minimum of about 30,000 US dollars. You can also try to upgrade to Amazon Retail Analytics Premium via Amazon Support. Navigate to Support in your Vendor central account. After entering your Business group, select the topic Reports - Amazon Retail Analytics and the Specific issue Upgrade to ARA Premium.

Once you have access to Amazon Retail Analytics, you can view the reports or download them as .csv files to browse later. This is a very useful feature, since it can take some time and more than a few sessions of mulling over the data before you can make the important decisions that will affect your business.

Some Disadvantages to Note

- Amazon Retail Analytics makes big claims about the data that it can provide, and it really is a lot of data. The reports do have their downsides, however, which are good to take note of.

- Both ARA Basic and the Premium version can be difficult to navigate and use at first. It will take quite a bit of time to learn how to get to each of them and how the reports work so you can get to the information that you need.

- Amazon makes use of third-party data providers, including vendors like yourself, to assemble all the data. This can be an issue for some, especially regarding data privacy.

- Amazon Retail Analytics is currently not capable of providing data on specific instances but rather presents trends over time.

- Some key information is not available on ARA reports, such as traffic sources and visitor paths. Even for vendors who use split testing, there is no way to see which campaign brought in the shoppers.

- ARA Premium shows the top 100 search terms for each Amazon department, but does not show vendors how many sessions or page views they have. The terms ranking is simply presented by popularity.

Amazon Retail Analytics may not be a perfect tool for measuring your Amazon business performance, but it can be a keen way of analyzing Amazon itself. Tools such as ARA Premium can give you an inside look at what Amazon expects and how you can adjust in areas like operations and optimization to rank higher on the platform. Amazon has its own formula, after all, and learning all that you can about it is what will spell success for your business.

ASIN Merging to Protect Your Brand & Grow Revenue

ASIN Merging is a powerful way that vendors (and sellers to an extent) can protect their brand on the Amazon platform and grow their visibility and sales at the same time. Often third-party sellers or resellers will attempt to list a vendor's product for sale on a separate ASIN. Most of the time they do this without knowing, but some will purposely create a separate ASIN. They may not be able to compete on pricing with Amazon or believe they can optimize the listing and still make money. The ASIN merging feature is a great way that vendors can fight these prohibited seller activities.

What are Prohibited Seller Activities?

Amazon created the Prohibited Sellers Activities and Actions policy to guide third-party sellers on what they can and cannot do with the platform. The policy is broad and covers a variety of different areas such as diverting customers from Amazon, manipulating customer feedback and reviews, manipulating your sales rank and inaccurate matching of products to the Amazon catalog.

This important part of the policy is broken into 3 parts. The first being that *"the product being offered must be listed on a product detail page that accurately describes the product in all respects."* Sellers cannot change product names or other attributes to make a product seem different than it really is. The next part is *"Creating a product detail page for a product already in the Amazon catalog is prohibited."* Duplicating listings is against Amazon's Terms of Service and if a seller creates a separate listing of your product (i.e., different ASIN) they are in violation of the policy. The final part is *"Sellers may not create separate listings for identical copies of the same item."* This means that if a product is sold in a 2-Pack a seller cannot create a separate 2-Pack listing. Amazon wants these policies followed tightly to prevent counterfeiting of their vendors' goods. Vendors can use this policy to protect their listings.

Increasing Revenue with ASIN Merging

Vendors can manage their catalog by using ASIN Merging in Vendor Central. When a third-party seller creates a duplicate listing for one of your products, you can contact Vendor Central and ask them to merge the listing with your listing. There is a template that can be used to submit the request, however Vendor support has indicated that a clear explanation in an email is also enough to have a listing merged.

Merging listings can be great for your account particularly if the third-party listing is performing well. With a merge, the third-party seller is now competing with Amazon on price point which is a losing battle for most sellers. Amazon will automatically recalculate their price to be lower than the third-party sellers within 24 hours to win the buy box back. Any review that was on the third party listing also becomes incorporated into your listing which can bring additional social proof to your product.

The largest benefit that you receive as a vendor is increased purchase orders from Amazon. We recently reviewed a new clients catalog and found multiple third-party listings that could be merged with our client's listings. The result of the merge is projected to be an additional $45,000 in monthly gross sales to Amazon, which translates roughly into $23,000 in additional purchase orders for our client every month.

Brand Gating to Protect Your Amazon Brand

Amazon has recently been making many updates to the Terms of Service for Amazon Sellers. One policy that went into effect on August 30th, 2016 was requiring Amazon approval to sell on certain product listings. The main purpose of this brand gating policy is to reduce the counterfeiting of goods from unscrupulous sellers, but it arguable has had the largest impact on third-party sellers and retail arbitragers selling genuine products. The new policy for sellers requires them to pay $1500 per brand, provide invoices from the manufacturer, and have written permission from the brand.

While this has negatively affected the ability of some third-party re-sellers, the clear winner is the brand owner. Brand owners can now implement a brand gating strategy to help boost their sales through Seller Central and limit the number of resellers on their listings.

Why is Brand Gating Important?

Brand gating is single-handedly the most effective way to protect your listings from hijackers. Hijackers (particularly from China) have been a challenge for sellers and in some instances have flooded product categories. Reducing counterfeiting is a huge focus area for Amazon and they have largely simplified the process. Previously, a seller was required to purchase the counterfeit goods to prove to Amazon how it did not match their product exactly. This got expensive for sellers that got flooded by hijackers and many gave up their listing.

The policy change provides sellers a proactive option to stop hijacking. Amazon has implemented this plan automatically to protect large brands like Nike. Individual sellers can request to have their brands gated on Amazon. The process may take a few weeks, but there are certain steps that you can follow to give your brand the best chance of being approved.

How to Get Your Brand Gated?

Follow these steps to give your brand the best chance of being gated. Amazon does not guarantee that they will accept the request – however they may move to more of an automatic brand gating process in the future. Here are the steps:

1. **Register Your Brand with Brand Registry:** Any seller must register their brand with brand registry in order to be considered a brand in Amazon's eyes. The process can be annoying as Amazon will push back on the smallest details. Amazon requires a few things to approve brand registry: a website, an email account hosted at the website and listed on the Amazon Seller Central account, images of the brand logo on the product and the packaging and the brand name. If you're missing any of these or there are slight differences, be prepared to see how frustrating Amazon makes this.

2. **Trademarking your brand (optional):** This step is optional, but can only help your case. It shows that you are actively interested in protecting your brand and can help in the approval process.

3. **List of ASINs for Brand Gating:** Amazon will need a list of your products that you want to be gated. They may gate your entire brand in some instances, but clearly indicating the listings to be gated will help move along the process.

4. **Highlight Your Counterfeiting Efforts:** Amazon does appear to give priority to sellers that are actively fighting counterfeiters on their listings. A history of removing counterfeiters will help you get your request approved. If you do not have a history,

discussing the other steps such as registering your brand and trademarking again shows that you take your brand serious.

5. **Providing Your Seller ID:** Indicate what your seller ID is to Amazon so the process goes smoothly.

It can take up to a month or more for a request to be approved. You may or may not receive an email notification from Amazon. To check if you brand gating request was approved, check your listings regularly. Click "Sell on Amazon" on your listing page in the "Other Sellers on Amazon" section. You will know if the request was approved if you are brought to a page saying "You need approval to list in this brand."

Understanding and Avoiding Amazon Chargebacks

Chargebacks are the silent killers of any Amazon business. They can throw a monkey wrench into nicely typed out revenue projections and reports. Instead of building those numbers, you end up with dollars leaking out the side because of errors and issues that can easily be avoided. Amazon chargebacks come for two main reasons, shipping and packaging. Compliance and operations checks can go a long way to prevent these chargebacks and stop your revenue leak.

Types of Amazon Chargebacks

You may be seeing deductions in your Remittance advice from Amazon and wonder why they are chipping away at your payments. Simply put, Amazon has a lot of rules, and when you don't comply with them, you get penalized to make up for their losses.

Amazon chargebacks fall into the main categories of shipping and packaging, and include anything from technical errors to missing barcodes to improper packing materials. Amazon chargebacks are operational non-compliance fees that stem directly from these errors and reflect as deductions on vendor remittance checks. Understand the types of Amazon chargebacks below to take the first step to getting back on track.

Purchase Order

The most common form of Amazon chargeback is errors related to purchase orders (POs). As little as failing to confirm a PO in a timely manner, shipping extra units or violating ship window policies can result in a chargeback. Vendors must confirm POs within 24 hours after releasing the order, and can only change the confirmation within 48 hours after this initial confirmation. They also should Accept or Back order within 24 hours via Vendor central or EDI. Back orders must have a ship window. Any failure in the above equates to an Amazon chargeback that can be quite large depending on the size of the order.

Package Transport

Amazon also files chargebacks when vendors fail to set up routing requests when they transport packages, or do not follow the correct policies for shipping and delivery fees. Vendors are required to create routing in advance of collect orders where Amazon pays the shipping charges. If the collect date is past the ship window a chargeback will follow.

Received Shipments

All shipments that arrive at Amazon Fulfillment Centers are checked for compliance. Any violations in the policies for shipments can mean another Amazon chargeback. These failures include labels on the boxes that do not have complete information, and barcodes that cannot be scanned or are missing altogether from the items and the carton labels.

Failure to meet shipping deadlines is also a chargeable offense. If the date of fulfillment is outside the ship window, a large chargeback can be expected. Orders that are not delivered within the specified period will be cancelled by Amazon, resulting in another sizeable chargeback for non-compliance.

Packaging

Amazon has very strict policies for the type of packaging that vendors must use when shipping product to them. Failing to polybag items or not bagging and taping items and cartons correctly are violations. Incorrect boxing, stuffing and bubble wrapping are also violations. Amazon will not hesitate to charge vendors for these mistakes. Failing to put the proper barcode or PO label on boxes – with the PO number – will also be a charge for vendors. Products that are close to expiry dates will also incur charges for vendors.

Advanced Ship Notice

Amazon requires that Advanced Ship Notice (ASN) be sent from Vendor Central or the EDI trading partner. Vendors must create the ASN in Vendor Central or through EDI before the shipments reach Amazon's Fulfillment Center. If the ASN is not sent by the vendor within two weeks of Receipt of the Shipment, fees will result. If the ASN is not sent correctly resulting in an error in transmitting the EDI, vendors will pay the price.

Avoid Amazon Chargebacks

It can be so frustrating for vendors to go through the rigorous process of becoming an Amazon vendor and then face chargebacks after all the price reductions that have already been suffered during negotiations. Vendors do get volume business from Amazon, but making mistakes is very costly. Even small mistakes on the part of a vendor can result in thousands in chargebacks. The good news is that you can avoid being slapped with Amazon chargebacks for service-related reasons. You can regain and improve your profitability by streamlining operations to meet compliance requirements.

Technical

- Process orders, acknowledge POs, etc. within the prescribed timeframe

- Send ASNs before PO's shipment is scanned in Amazon FC via manual entry in Vendor Central on the ship date or instruct your EDI provider to check Amazon's 856 mapping

- Create routing requests for shipment collect orders before sending PO shipments to Amazon

- Consider an EDI system to automate order processing, including acknowledgment, ASNs, and instruct EDI provider to check 855 PO Acknowledgment mapping

- Enter correct shipping dates for different units within 12 hours, including on weekends

- Develop a system for checking and tracking product expiry

Packaging

- Label your packages correctly with correctly printed labels and clear barcodes

- Follow packing guidelines for bagging, bubble wrapping, taping, etc.

- Check packing issues at the Distribution Center level

- Check ASIN information on labels printed from Vendor Central

- Advise EDI provider to check GS1 Label mapping for Amazon

- Review Amazon Packaging Certifications Guidelines in the Vendor Central Resource Center to comply operationally

Shipping

- Don't change the shipping address that has been provided by Amazon

- Choose a shipping method that provides tracking and delivery confirmation for high value merchandise

- Do not ship either before or after the ship window

- Keep clear shipping records with shipping dates, method, tracking, receipt, and photo evidence of labels and other requirements for 6 months after the order date

- If units are unavailable by ship cancel date, cancel units from PO and ship what is available

- Consider requesting your Amazon buyer to give wider PO shipment windows or send POs on Monday mornings only

Find a Chargeback on Vendor Central

If you are facing a chargeback, you can review the details in the Payments tab of your Vendor Central account in one of two ways:

1. Navigate to Remittance and check the itemized deductions listed under the Description for the check that includes the Amazon chargeback.

2. Navigate to Vendor Operational Performance to see all charge types and totals for your account in the past year, particularly operational errors. Select an Amazon chargeback type from the list to learn about the details.

Knowing what the chargeback is for will help you identify what to avoid in the future. The details on amount, status, and type will also help you manage the chargeback or a dispute if you feel that the charges are erroneous.

Dealing with Chargebacks

The process of Amazon chargebacks begins when a buyer requests a chargeback from their credit card company. The credit card company contacts Amazon to obtain the details of the transaction in question. Amazon Payments sends the vendor an email notification to request this information. If you have received such a notification, you may issue a refund or dispute the chargeback with the credit card company through Amazon.

Whichever way you decide to go, you must respond to the notification within 7 days, including weekends, or the chargeback will be automatically approved. Make sure that you also respond promptly to any other requests relating to the chargeback. Check your Vendor Operational Performance page frequently to avoid missing the deadline on any new chargebacks.

Filing a Dispute

If you decide to dispute an Amazon chargeback, you must familiarize yourself with the details of the chargeback. Prepare any records related to the chargeback in support of your claim. You must present these and craft a clear and concise explanation of why you are disputing the chargeback to have any chance of getting it cleared. You will typically have to provide information such as the shipped date, shipping method, tracking, and item information. Make sure that you are also following all the terms of your Vendor Agreement.

If you are facing several disputes, create separate documentation and explanations for each of them to increase your chances of approval. When you are ready to file, navigate to the Represent your case link on the Performance page under Chargeback Claims.

Once you have filed your dispute, keep checking for updates so that you can respond in a timely manner. You can see whether the dispute is under review, needs more information, is approved, is paid, or denied. Pay close attention to information needed so that you can prepare and provide supporting documents quickly. You have only 30 days' total to process your dispute. If your dispute is denied, read the reasons carefully. You are allowed only one more chance to dispute and provide more evidence. In most cases where clear evidence is provided, Amazon will approve your dispute and you will find the deducted amount credited back to your account within 90 days.

Transitioning from being an Amazon Vendor to a Third-Party Seller

There are quite a lot of vendors who want to shift from being a vendor to a third-party seller on Amazon. Being a vendor has its advantages. The lure of more control over the entire selling process versus having Amazon call all the shots, however, is a strong one. The attraction is pulling many towards the move to becoming a third-party seller. It is always possible for a vendor to opt for a shift, and this shift does not always have to be a complete change. Vendors must think carefully about this decision, though. There is a process and a few considerations that can affect a brand's decision to make the change.

Vendor Versus Third Party Seller

Vendors sell to Amazon and not to customers. Amazon will decide how much of each product they want to sell. Amazon will also decide how much they want certain products to sell for. This will affect the price offered for your inventory, wholesale. You can appeal for better numbers before signing your agreement with the platform, or by going through a contract renegotiation. Ultimately, however, Amazon holds the power in this relationship and will accept or reject your proposed terms. This is the extent of a vendor's control over products. Once the wholesale exchange has been made, the products belong to Amazon and Amazon has complete control over them, marked as sold by Amazon and shipped by Amazon.

Third party sellers on Amazon maintain ownership over the products that they sell on the platform. They therefore have control of all aspects of the process, apart from the platform regulations that they must comply with. Being a seller is of course a lot more responsibility, and so the decision to switch over must not be taken lightly. Sellers are responsible for all aspects of the business, from inventory that doesn't sell to marketing to customer complaints.

#1 – Inventory

The Ships and Sold By Amazon.com label can be an advantage for vendors. Online shoppers have a high level of trust in the online retail giant, and will continue to buy from Amazon because the company is built on a foundation of excellent customer care. As more customers buy the products that you sell to Amazon, your relationship with the platform as a vendor will solidify, providing you with a steady source of income.

Third party sellers have control over how much product they want to sell on Amazon. They are selling directly to Amazon customers and are at liberty to increase or decrease inventory at will. They are also free to add new products to offer on Amazon, provided of course that these products are permitted on the platform and meet Amazon's high standards. This freedom is a major factor for the growth of any Amazon business.

Vendors do not have a very good chance of pushing new products through without allowing Amazon the chance to sell a sample of these products first. Launching a new product via Vendor Central is a tricky business since Amazon can end up giving you a low price offering for a product that you know will become a big hit. Again, you can try to renegotiate the terms of your agreement with Amazon after they have realized the product's potential, but there is no guarantee that Amazon will share a piece of the pie with you.

As a third-party seller, you can launch your new products as you wish, with whatever marketing methods you deem fit, and price and reprice them as you like in line with your launch campaign and as the product gains popularity. Sellers can also take advantage of advertising tools that provide them with the data that they need to encourage conversions and gain recognition from Amazon for better rankings on the platform. Third party sellers now have the whole pie, and can entice Amazon to buy the product or continue selling it exclusively.

One distinct advantage of deciding to branch out into third party selling is taking advantage of stockouts. It often happens that Amazon will make a purchase order for a product from a vendor but then sell out before another order can be made. As a vendor-seller, you can take advantage of these instances by having the out of stock product available when Amazon runs out.

It is important to note here that third party sellers are often unable to compete with Amazon pricing. This means that Amazon will usually win out every time where pricing alone is concerned. It would not be a good business decision to rely solely on Amazon stockouts for certain products. Sellers can, however, provide additional value to customers in various ways to win back and maintain a fair share of the customer base on top of the occasional stockout.

#2 – Pricing and Promotions

Vendors have no control over how much Amazon will sell the products that they have wholesaled to the platform. They also have no control over how these products will be marketed and promoted.

Sellers have more control over how they price their products. Successful third party sellers must certainly consider the pricing of the competition before they list exorbitant rates. At the end of the day, however, is a seller has a truly unique product with a lot of value, the price can be as high as they want it to be – as high as the market can tolerate. Sellers also have complete control over any promotions that they want to offer to customers, and how often they want to do this. There are more Amazon regulations regarding promotions, such as the recent ban on requesting reviews in exchange for free products or discounts.

Third party sellers are free, however, to promote their products by all available means on Amazon, and on other platforms as well.

#3 – Listing

Amazon knows best how to optimize listings to rank on their own platform, and products sold by Amazon are certainly at the top of the charts. Vendors can ride this wave as the Amazon products become popular and demand increases. The contents of all listings are created by Amazon based on the information requested from vendors. Vendors have no control over what Amazon decides to out there, though.

Sellers have complete control over the information that they choose to include on their listings, again, as long as it complies with Amazon's terms. Sellers certainly know much more about their products than Amazon does, and this allows sellers to better communicate the products' value to customers. This is another distinct advantage of choosing to do a partial switch from vendor to third party seller.

#4 – Customers

Vendors have no contact with the end customers. Amazon takes care of the entire process from marketing and shipping the products to providing customer service.

Sellers can choose how much contact they wish to have with their customers. They must maintain a high customer satisfaction rating to remain competitive on Amazon, of course, but they choose how they communicate with their customers and how often. This open line of communication provides third party sellers with the distinct advantage of being in control of their relationship with customers. The quality, tone and depth of this relationship is important to the growth of any business, but more so on a platform like Amazon that puts so much emphasis on customer loyalty. Sellers can answer product inquiries more precisely with their in-depth knowledge of their products, can develop a more defined brand personality that speaks directly to customers, and deal directly with all concerns that affect their product and brand.

Amazon Blocks

As a last note, although any vendor can technically switch over to third party selling, Amazon does prevent some vendors from moving over to selling. Amazon has a vested interest in maintaining their established vendor relationships. Having a good vendor relationship with Amazon is of course also advantageous. Amazon sees these switches not as positive expansions, however, but as business being taken away from them. If Amazon prefers to keep you as a vendor exclusively, they have the power to prevent you from entering the seller side, whether the switch is partial or full.

CONCLUSION

At this point you should be aware of how incredibly fast Amazon is growing. The new opportunities afforded by this growth need to be harnessed by every company looking for long-term growth. Amazon will continue to expand and open new avenues to sellers and vendors. Implementing our blueprint or working with us will create a powerful sales channel for your business. We hope our expertise will guide you to success on Amazon.

We've made this book to provide as much information as possible about how we grow our clients' sales. Our blueprint has led to massive growth for our customers, and implementing the same strategies can help you grow as well. This guide will require some testing and experimenting on your part to discover what strategies work the best for your business. Expect that you will face failures or obstacles as you begin to refine and harness the power of these strategies. Do not quit on these strategies quickly when these challenges arise. Use them as opportunities to grow, expand upon and refine our advice to work for you.

We hope that you have enjoyed learning more about the Amazon platform and our blueprint for success. The opportunity to grow on, and with, the Amazon platform are almost unlimited. Our hope is that these strategies change the course of your company and business forever. Thank you for giving us the opportunity to help you realize your brand's eCommerce potential.

We understand that implementing many of the strategies in this book may be a challenge for business owners to focus on. We strongly believe that focusing on your strengths and finding others to compliment your weaknesses is the best way to grow. If you need help implementing any of the strategies that we have mentioned in this book, please reach out to us at www.amzadvisers.com. Take advantage of what you have learned and take your business to the next level on Amazon today!

List of Resources

Google Keyword Planner
Free keyword research tool that can provide valuable insight to high traffic keywords on the Google Search Engine
www.adwords.google.com/KeywordPlanner

Keyword Inspector
A keyword research tool developed for Amazon sellers that focuses on finding the keywords that customers use while searching for a product or niche
www.keywordinspector.com

Sellics
A suite of tools that offers a free trial and is designed to help research keywords, optimize listings and grow your business
www.sellics.com

Jungle Scout
A powerful research tool that extrapolates Amazon marketplace data to provide insights into monthly sales, revenue and best seller rankings based on keyword searches
www.junglescout.com

AMZ Tracker
A suite of tools to help you research products, track competitors and optimize your listings
www.amztracker.com

Feedback Genius
An automated email tool that integrates with Amazon to send specific emails to customers at pre-arranged time periods to increase product

reviews and seller feedbacks
www.feedbackgenius.com

Salesbacker
Another automated email tool designed to increase your product reviews and seller feedbacks over time
www.salesbacker.com

Kibly
A program partnered with Amazon to automate emails to customers and gain more reviews for your products
www.kibly.com

Shopify
One of the fastest growing and most popular eCommerce store front website hosting programs that can be integrated with Amazon accounts to allow customers quick purchases
www.shopify.com

Wordpress
An easy to use interface to build custom stores utilizing WooCommerce or other plug-ins
www.wordpress.org

BigCommerce
An all-in-one eCommerce platform that allows your store to connect Amazon accounts for quick customer purchases
www.bigcommerce.com

Freeeup
An outsourcing business that has affordable, highly skilled workers to help you focus on growing your business
www.freeeup.com

Upwork
A website for freelancers with all types of skills that can help you affordably outsource work
www.upwork.com

TaxJar
A program that integrates with Amazon and tracks all the sales tax that you are required to pay for each sale on the platform
www.taxjar.com

38215486R00077

Printed in Great Britain
by Amazon